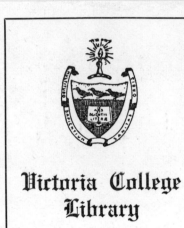

Carnegie Endowment for International Peace
DIVISION OF INTERNATIONAL LAW

The Status of the
International Court of Justice

WITH AN APPENDIX OF ADDRESSES AND
OFFICIAL DOCUMENTS

BY

JAMES BROWN SCOTT, A.M., J.U.D., LL.D.

*Member of the Institute of International Law; Technical Delegate of
the United States to the Second Hague Peace Conference;
Lecturer on International Law and Diplomacy
in Johns Hopkins University*

NEW YORK
OXFORD UNIVERSITY PRESS
AMERICAN BRANCH: 35 WEST 32ND STREET
LONDON, TORONTO, MELBOURNE, AND BOMBAY
HUMPHREY MILFORD
1916

THE QUINN & BODEN CO. PRESS
RAHWAY, N. J.

PREFACE

" As is well known, the American delegation to the Second Peace Conference was directed by Mr. Root, as Secretary of State, to present a proposal for an International Court of Justice. Germany and Great Britain approved the plan and a joint project of the three nations was laid before the Conference. France, although not technically a party, warmly supported the idea. A draft convention concerning the Court, which by this time was known as the Court of Arbitral Justice, was adopted by the Conference and its establishment recommended through diplomatic channels.

" It seems to the officers of the American Society for Judicial Settlement of International Disputes that the time has come for a somewhat elaborate account of the present status of the proposal, so that the partisans of judicial settlement shall be informed not only as to the original proposition, but as to the steps which have been taken to realize it. Documents too long for quotation in the article have been included in an appendix, which will, it is hoped, be found a useful supplement to the statements contained in the text and place before the reader the material necessary for a correct understanding of the draft convention adopted by the Second Conference, and the process by which that fortunate result was reached."

Such was the preface to the tractate published but a few weeks (to be accurate, in the month of July) before the outbreak of the great war in August 1914. The Honorable Elihu Root felt justified in saying in a letter to the undersigned that " It is very clear and satisfactory and it came at just the right time, because on all these subjects we shall have to take a new departure after the war, and this paper is a summing up of the status of peaceable settlement

iii

at the close of the period.   It ought to be in permanent book form."
With the permission of the Judicial Settlement Society, of which
the undersigned is Secretary, the original pamphlet now appears
" in permanent book form," without a change of any kind, unless it
be the correction of a typographical error.

JAMES BROWN SCOTT,
Director of the Division of International Law.

WASHINGTON, D. C.,
February 28, 1916.

CONTENTS

The Status of the International Court of Justice

When the American delegation, acting under specific instructions from Mr. Elihu Root, at that time Secretary of State, proposed to the Second Peace Conference, held at The Hague in 1907, the creation of a truly permanent international court of justice, the proposal, which had long been cherished by enlightened thinkers, ceased to be academic; for a country, not the least respected in the society of nations, had not only confessed its faith publicly in the feasibility of such an institution and the services which it could render, but had actually called upon the nations in conference assembled to co-operate in its establishment. The idea was neither new nor novel; but its submission by a government to an international conference was an event of no mean magnitude. The delegates were skeptical and expressed misgivings; but when Germany and Great Britain united in a project for the creating of such a court, with the loyal and unquestioning support of France, it was apparent that the proposal would have to be reckoned with.

As the result of weeks—indeed months—of discussion, in which the friends and the foes of the new institution expressed their views, a draft convention of thirty-five articles was adopted, providing for the organization, the jurisdiction, and the procedure of the tribunal, which by this time had come to be known as the Court of Arbitral Justice. The draft was and still remains a torso, because of the inability of the Conference to agree upon a method generally satisfactory of appointing the judges; but it was felt that this objection, however serious it might be, was one which time could remove, and the Conference remitted this question to the channels of diplomacy, recommending "to the Signatory Powers the project * * * of a convention for the establishment of a Court of Arbitral Justice and its execution as soon as an agreement should be reached upon the choice of judges and the constitution of the Court."

If we bear in mind the difficulties, apparently insurmountable, which stood in the way of the creation of the Permanent Court of Arbitration by the First Hague Conference, it is evident that a proposal to create a permanent International Court of Justice would have been rejected, if it had been laid before that august assemblage. That it was favorably considered and an agreement reached upon its institution by the Second Conference shows the progress that had been made in the interval, even although the temple of justice lacked the final touches, as it came from the builders' hands. Time is the great ally of progress, and there is every reason to believe that, if not definitely constituted in the interval between the second and the third conference, public opinion will enable the Third Conference to complete the structure.

The State of Opinion To-day. The situation to-day is very different from that which existed when the proposal was made to the Second Conference. It would be unfair to say that the need or usefulness of an international court of justice had not been discussed; but it is strictly within the truth to assert that it had not been considered by what we are pleased to call practical men, much less by statesmen in office. Now and then, and here and there, a publicist had proposed the creation of such an institution; but the plan fell, as it were, stillborn. The publicists generally did not take it up and did not treat it seriously. The influence, however, of the Hague Conference is so great and its recommendations so persuasive that what had been looked upon as Utopian was seen to have the germs of possibility within it. Individual publicists, professors of international law, learned societies, and men of affairs now consider the proposed Court not merely as feasible but as essential to the world's progress. A sentiment has been created in its behalf, and this sentiment, largely concentrated in the United States, has made its way, to use a theological expression, *in partibus infidelium*.

The burden of proof has shifted or is shifting, and the opponent of the institution feels required to justify his opposition and not the partisan his faith. It is not suggested that the battle is won, for much remains to be done. It is believed, however, that forces have been called into being which will result in ultimate victory, and it may be said, almost without fear of contradiction, that what was the hope of the few has become the conviction of the many, and that the sentiment confined to localities is becoming the prevailing opinion of nations. The presentation of the proposal by the American delegation to and its adoption by the Second Conference was an international event. The establishment of the Court is a matter of international policy, and its success seems only to be a question of time; for even although its creation be delayed and although many of its partisans now living may not see it called into being, the years that will in any event elapse before it administers justice between nations, while important to the individual, are as nothing in the lives of nations.

Reasons for and Objects of Its Proposals. In view of these circumstances it seems well to state, however briefly and imperfectly, the reasons which have led to its proposal, the arguments which have been advanced for its creation, the services which it is believed that it will render to the society of nations, and to make clear the present status of the proposition.

The first article of the draft convention referred to states within the compass of a single paragraph, and in clear and unmistakable terms, not merely the aims and purposes of the advocates of a permanent court of international justice, but also its relation to the so-called Permanent Court of Arbitration. "With a view," it is said, "of promoting the cause of arbitration, the contracting powers agree to constitute, without altering the status of the Permanent Court of Arbitration, a court of arbitral justice of free and easy access, composed of judges representing the various juridical systems of the world and capable of insuring continuity in arbitral jurisprudence." As the full import of this article will be explained later, it is not deemed advisable to comment upon it here further than to say that a permanent court was contemplated to be composed of judges not appointed for the particular case to be decided, but selected at the time of constituting the court. The judges were to be chosen in such a way that they would bring to the performance of their duty both knowledge and experience acquired by years of training in different legal systems. By reason of the permanency of the judges so chosen, it was felt that there would be continuity in their decisions, with the result that international law would be developed by its judgments, just as national law is developed by the decisions of national courts. Finally, it was meant to be free and easy of access, that is to say, open to the contracting nations as national courts are open to litigants, and easy of access because it would be an existing court, not one whose judges would need to be chosen for each case submitted to it.

Such is in briefest terms the proposal of the delegations of Germany, the United States, and Great Britain, a proposal concurred in by the French delegation, although it was not a party to the project when originally presented. It will be observed, and the matter is mentioned here by reason of its importance, that the Permanent Court of Arbitration devised by the First Hague Conference is not to be altered. It is to exist, and is not to be supplanted by the newer institution. The nations are to choose one or the other, according to the nature of the controversy, or according to their sovereign pleasure. The question naturally presents itself: What progress has been made toward its establishment? But, as the proposition could not have been made in 1907 unless the principle of arbitration had been accepted by the nations so as to suggest the need of a permanent court in which to pass upon and decide controversies arising between nations, it seems advisable to trace briefly the movement in favor of arbitration which, beginning with the Jay Treaty of 1794, between Great Britain and the United States, culminated at the First Hague Conference by the creation of the so-called Permanent Court and the Code of Arbitral Procedure, contained in the Convention for the Pacific Settlement of International Disputes, adopted by the Conference, and since accepted by the nations at large.

It will also be necessary to consider the provisions of the Permanent Court of Arbitration, its advantages, which are many, and its defects, which are grave, before taking up in detail the proposed court of international justice.

Previous History of Movement in Favor of Arbitration. Two extracts from two distinguished European publicists, the one written during the throes of the French Revolution, and the other after the close of the revolutionary wars and the fall of the Empire, will perhaps best show the state of mind obtaining at these two periods. The first, George Friedrich von Martens, justly regarded as one of the founders of international law, said of arbitration, that " this measure, much used during the whole of the Middle Ages, has not been entirely abandoned up to the present day, but the examples of arbitration offered and accepted have become rare, and more rare from an experience of the drawbacks which seem to be inseparable from this method, which is ordinarily insufficient, especially because of the lack of an executive power." The second writer, likewise a German publicist of distinction and, like Martens, a man of wide experience and of broad knowledge, said " this method has been almost entirely neglected for several centuries. To judge by the manifestoes and proclamations, a sovereign never made war except in spite of himself, and after having done and tried everything to prevent it. Why do we not return to arbitration? At most we accept the mediation of a third power, but this is usually ineffective. There is no longer anything but war, so to speak, which can insure the inviolability of the laws."

If, however, the outlook upon the Continent was dark and apparently hopeless, Great Britain and its vigorous offspring on the other side of the Atlantic had already resorted to arbitration for the settlement of their outstanding disputes and had brought again into the practice of nations the agency of peaceful settlement which in the past hundred years has been so productive of beneficial results. To understand the reasons which led Great Britain and the United States to agree to submit their existing disputes to arbitration and, by inserting arbitral clauses in the Jay Treaty, " to return to arbitrators," to employ the language of Klüber, it is advisable to premise some general observations.

First, as to Great Britain. While it is true that Mr. Jay negotiated the treaty with Lord Grenville, at that time Secretary of Foreign Affairs, it is believed that Mr. Pitt's Cabinet was inclined to arbitration because of the presence in it of the first Lord Liverpool, who was president of the Board of Trade and Chancellor of the Duchy of Lancaster: an expert in commercial matters, and an unhesitating and outspoken advocate of arbitration. In a work published in 1785 and entitled " A General Collection of Treaties Between Great Britain and Other Powers from 1648 to 1783," His

Lordship called particular attention to the arbitral treaties concluded by Cromwell. He mentions them as " of a piece with all the rest of Cromwell's negotiations," and " that they speak so well for themselves as not to need illustration." As his toryism was unquestioned, Lord Liverpool must indeed have been a convinced partisan of arbitration, for in those days commendation of Cromwell was far from popular and almost treasonable in official circles. Nevertheless Lord Liverpool felt justified in saying that Cromwell's treaties of arbitration " illustrate the bright side of this man, who, in the light these particulars shew him, is worthy of imitation; therefore those who write or speak of him with an invidious warmth should consider, if these facts be true and they cannot shew the same in behalf of their favorite kings, what a terrible sarcasm it is upon them that a man whom they vilify and abuse is proved to have been infinitely wiser and honester than either such kings or their advocates; and consequently, in abusing him, express their contempt for virtue, and at the same time make their kings less estimable than the person whom they would have wicked beyond expression."

It is to be presumed that in negotiations of a commercial character the views and the advice of the president of the Board of Trade would exercise no little influence upon his colleague, the Secretary of State for Foreign Affairs.

Next, as to the United States. If Franklin is to be taken as representing public opinion, it is clear that in the earliest days of our history there was not only a strong sentiment in favor of peaceful settlement, but in favor of arbitration and of judicial decision of what may be considered international disputes. For whatever may now be the position of the states of the American Union, there can be little doubt that during the Revolution and under the Articles of Confederation they regarded themselves as little less than sovereign, and that they considered controversies between them as disputes between sovereignties.

In the midst of the American Revolution, Franklin wrote: " We make daily great improvement in natural, there is one I hope to see in moral, philosophy—the discovery of a plan which will induce and oblige nations to settle their disputes without first cutting one another's throats." And in the following passage he pointed out the method which has prevented " the throat cutting " to which he and his kind objected:

" When will mankind be convinced that all wars are follies, very expensive, and very mischievous, and agree to settle their differences by arbitration? "

The plan which he had in mind was the arbitration of international disputes instead of their adjustment by force, and the reduction of armament by compact. It may be admitted that the good doctor was ahead of his time, but not so far ahead as to question his standing as a practical man of affairs. Again, the United States in Congress assembled was in favor of the peaceable, indeed judicial, settlement of international controversies; and naturally so, because the charters of the different colonies frequently overlapped, and the states were unwilling to renounce what the colonies had claimed. Diplomatic adjustment by commissioners was frequently resorted to, but failed to commend itself in the long run. Therefore the Congress provided in the Articles of Confederation a method of settling disputes between the confederated states, which are expressly declared to be sovereign, by special tribunals or commissions, the commissioners or judges of which should be chosen for the particular case for the settlement of " all disputes and differences now subsisting or that hereafter may arise between two or more states concerning boundary, jurisdiction, or any other cause whatever." The method as tried by the temporary commission did not, as in the case of diplomatic adjustment, commend itself. It was, therefore, replaced by a permanent court, namely, the Supreme Court of the United States, which was invested with the jurisdiction formerly conferred by the Ninth Article upon temporary commissions. At the time, therefore, of Jay's Treaty mixed commissions had been created to pass upon and to determine disputes between the states; and finally, a permanent tribunal had been created by the Constitution for the judicial decision of controversies between the states and which has constantly and satisfactorily settled disputes between the states. It was natural, therefore, that the statesmen of the young republic should look with a friendly eye upon arbitration or judicial settlement when diplomacy had failed to settle international controversies.

But we are not without positive knowledge and we do not need to resort to conjecture. The American negotiator of the Treaty of 1794 was John Jay, and the treaty appropriately bears his name. He had been Secretary of State for Foreign Affairs under the Confederacy, and held that office under the Constitution until he was succeeded by Mr. Jefferson. He was the first Chief Justice of the Supreme Court. As Secretary of State for Foreign Affairs he recommended arbitration, and as Chief Justice he was fortunate enough to put his recommendation into effect. As Secretary of State he sent a report, dated April 21, 1785, to Congress, recommending that " an effective measure should immediately be taken to settle all disputes with the Crown of Great Britain," respecting the northeastern boundary of the United States. He suggested that the papers in the case " should be transmitted to the Minister Plenipotentiary of the United States at that Court, with instructions to present a proper representation of the case and to propose that commissioners be appointed to hear and finally decide the disputes." The report not merely advises that the disputes be referred to commissioners; it contains all necessary details concerning their appointment and the procedure to be followed by them.

No action appears to have been taken by Congress upon this epoch-making proposal; and when President Washington assumed office under the Constitution, the disputes with Great Britain were still outstanding. Mr. Jay had been appointed Chief Justice, but, as has been said, he acted as Secretary of State until Mr. Jefferson assumed the office upon his return from France. Therefore, doubtless upon the recommendation of Mr. Jay, President Washington sent, under date of February 9, 1790, to the first Congress under the Constitution a copy of Jay's report, stating not merely that " it is desirable that all questions " with Great Britain but that " all questions between this and any other nations be speedily and amicably settled." It is to be observed that Jay's original recommendation that disputes with Great Britain be settled by commissions was enlarged and broadened in its scope so as to include " all questions between this and any other nations," by President Washington, who knew from actual experience in the field, as Jay did not, the hardships of war. But this is not all. To be settled amicably, Washington knew that they should be speedily settled, because trifling disputes may become by delay and mismanagement grave political issues. We are thus in a position to understand why the United States proposed arbitration, and why Great Britain accepted it.

The Congress under the Constitution, like the Congress under the Confederation, failed to take action, but the stirring events of the French Revolution, the causes of friction that daily arose between Great Britain and the United States, convinced President Washington that the two nations were rapidly drifting into war, which could only be averted by a treaty between the two countries which would settle outstanding difficulties. Naturally, he turned to Jay, and the Chief Justice did not fail him. He accepted the mission to England; he negotiated the treaty which bears his name, and which is an imperishable monument to his wisdom and humanity, his patriotism, and self-sacrifice. He preserved peace; he introduced into the practice of nations the greatest agency for maintaining peace; but he sacrificed, as he knew he would, his political career. In the Senate the treaty was mutilated and was only advised and consented to by a narrow margin. The appropriations necessary to put it into effect were carried by a majority of three in the House of Representatives. Jay was burned in effigy and both Jay and his treaty were damned from one end of the country to the other. It is a fact, however, that Jay's reputation as a benefactor of his kind rests upon the firm foundations of this treaty, and that the policy of the United States in its very beginning in the matter of arbitration and peaceful settlement was determined by him. The articles of Jay's treaty dealing with arbitration are three in number—the fifth, sixth and seventh, to which may be added the eighth, relating to expenses. The fifth refers to the final decision of the commissioners the determination of the St. Croix River, forming a part of the boundary between the two countries; the sixth, concerning the losses and damages to British creditors by reason of impediments interposed to the recovery of debts; and the seventh submitted to commissioners the losses alleged to have been incurred by British and American merchants by reason of the illegal captures of their vessels and property by Great Britain and the United States respectively. The success of the commission under the seventh article showed the feasibility of arbitration, and the decisions of this commission are considered classics of international arbitration.

In the hundred years following Jay's treaty many and important cases have been submitted to arbitration by nations other than Great Britain and the United States. Although these two countries are still the leaders, as they were the beginners, it is estimated that there have been some two hundred submissions, and often the submission as in the case of the Claims Convention of 1853, between Great Britain and the United States, involved many cases. From this point of view the cases, as distinguished from the agreements, have been numerous, and nations have had ample opportunity of testing arbitration.

As the result of this experience, two things were seen to be necessary or advisable: the one a code of international procedure, and the other more adequate machinery for the trial and determination of the cases. Indeed, it may be said that the wisdom of a third had become evident, for in order that arbitration may bring forth its good fruits it is essential that nations agree by a formal instrument, or in a clause of a general treaty, to submit their controversies to arbitration. The agreement to refer existing differences is hard to reach, whereas it is a comparatively simple matter to conclude a treaty, binding the contracting parties to submit future disputes to arbitration. The advantage of this is evident, because nations are not in the frame of mind to submit disputes which perhaps have ruffled their friendly relations, whereas they feel bound to submit them if there is an agreement concluded in times of good feeling which requires them to arbitrate when and as they arise. The special treaty or clause submitting existing disputes has been supplemented by the general treaty or the general clause, binding their good faith to submit their disputes generally or certain categories of them to arbitration. This innovation is due, it would seem, to William Jay, the son of John Jay, and his successor in the good work. In a tractate published in 1842, entitled " War and Peace: The Evils of the First and a Plan for Preserving the Last," William Jay urged the United States to include the following article in its treaties:

" It is agreed between the contracting parties that if, unhappily, any controversy shall hereafter arise between them in respect to the true meaning and intention of any stipulation in this present treaty, or in respect to any other subject, which controversy cannot be satisfactorily adjusted by negotiation, neither party shall resort to hostilities against the other; but the matter in dispute shall, by a special convention, be submitted to the arbitrament of one or more friendly powers; and the parties hereby agree to abide by the award which may be given in pursuance of such submission."

He singled out France because no rivalry existed between it and the United States, and he foresaw "no prospect of an interruption of that harmony which has so long marked the intercourse of the two nations." If he had the harmlessness of the dove, he likewise had the wisdom of the serpent, because he both felt and knew that it would be easier to negotiate such a treaty with France than with any other nation, and he foresaw that the experience with one nation would inevitably result in the very general introduction of the proposed article. In this he has not been disappointed, and it is a matter of great comfort to those who believe that the ultimate triumph should be traced to its modest source to note that the first general treaty of arbitration concluded by the United States was negotiated in 1908 by Mr. Root, worthy in every way of the Jays, with, as Mr. Jay suggested, "our first and ancient ally"—France.

We are thus to-day surrounded, as it were, with a network of treaties of arbitration, and it is almost as true of the son as it was of the father that he builded better than he knew.

But supposing that general or special treaties existed, it would be of inestimable advantage to nations in controversy to have for their guidance a code of arbitral procedure which they could vary to meet the special needs of the occasion if they did not care to adopt it and to apply it in its entirety. And it is not the least service of that enlightened body of publicists composing the Institute of International Law that they recognized the need of such a code, foresaw its applicability, and drafted its provisions. Within a year after its organization, in 1873, the Institute prepared a code which, subsequently amended, served as the basis of all future discussion, and was adopted substantially by the First Hague Conference.

But another step required to be taken to facilitate the recourse to arbitration. The Jay Treaty provided for the appointment of temporary commissions to be composed of commissioners chosen by the two governments, and subsequent treaties have likewise provided for temporary commissions or tribunals to be composed of persons chosen by the two governments to decide the matters submitted to them. It was felt that it would be a great help to the nations if a general agreement were reached upon the constitution of the tribunals and if the names of appropriate persons were called to the attention of the nations from whom the desired number could be chosen to form the tribunal. The Interparliamentary Union, due to the initiative of an enlightened Englishman, the late Sir Randal Cremer, proposed at its session of 1894 at The Hague the creation of a permanent international court, and a year later a definite project was adopted at Brussels.

Without going into detail, it is sufficient to state that the court contemplated by the Union was to be a large and permanent body, as each nation was to possess the right to appoint two arbiters, although it was provided that two or more nations could unite and jointly appoint the two members in question. They were to serve for a period of five years and might be reappointed. The court was to sit in a particular locality to be agreed upon; its members were to receive salaries by the states appointing them, and the expenses of the court as such were to be paid equally by the states constituting it.

As in the case of the Code of Arbitral Procedure, so in the case of the Permanent Court of Arbitration, it is evident that the First Hague Conference found material at hand which it could use if the delegates were minded to facilitate the recourse to arbitration, and it is the crowning glory of the Conference that, notwithstanding the opposition of Germany, it was so minded, and that it made a high use of the projects which such an enlightened body as the Institute of International Law and such an influential body as the Interparliamentary Union had thought out, prepared and drafted.

We are now prepared to understand the action of the First Hague Conference on Arbitration, Arbitral Procedure, and the Court of Arbitration.

Sketch of the Present Movement. In the month of August, 1898, the present enlightened Czar of Russia invited the governments accredited to the Court of St. Petersburg to appoint delegates to a conference; and the powers having consented, a second circular was issued a few months later in the nature of a program. For the present purpose, the following paragraph may be quoted, requesting the powers in conference "to accept in principle the employment of good offices, of mediation and facultative arbitration in cases lending themselves thereto, with the object of preventing armed conflicts between nations; to come to an understanding with respect to the mode of applying these good offices, and to establish a uniform practice in using them."

It will be observed that while arbitration is mentioned, the understanding to be reached related to good offices. The Conference, however, broadened the scope of this article, and not merely approved arbitration, but came to an understanding with respect to the mode of applying arbitration, and secured, to paraphrase the article, a uniform practice in using it. The American delegation seems to have been the only one instructed by a government to propose a court of arbitration. It appears, however, from a very interesting address before the Judicial Settlement Society in 1913, made by the Hon. David Jayne Hill, formerly Ambassador to Germany, and at the time of the First Conference Assistant Secretary of State of the United States, that the proposal for the court came, not from the United States, but from Sir Julian Pauncefote, British Ambassador to the United States, in order to insure the success of the Conference, which at that time was problematical. As it is evident, however, that a court of arbitration presupposed an agreement to resort to arbitration, and that the resort would be facilitated by the adoption of a code of procedure for the guidance of the court when established, the Conference took action on both these matters, as appears from the following articles of the Convention for the Pacific Settlement of International Disputes:

"International arbitration has for its object the settlement of differences between states by judges of their own choice, and on the basis of respect for law." (Article 15.)

It will be noted that this is a general statement, defining the object and the method, but not necessarily approving arbitration. The next article, however, puts the stamp of approval on arbitration:

"In questions of a legal nature, and especially in the interpretation or application of International Conventions, arbitration is recognized by the Signatory Powers as the most effective, and at the same time the most equitable, means of settling disputes which diplomacy has failed to settle." (Article 16.)

Direct negotiation is here regarded, if not the best, nevertheless as the first means of settling international disputes, and, upon its failure, arbitration is stated by the Conference to be the most effective and equitable means of settling a dispute after the failure of diplomacy. It will be observed that the approval, however, is restricted to disputes of a legal nature, and that as pre-eminently legal, the interpretation and application of international conventions are singled out. This modest, and indeed hesitating, approbation of a method which had been more broadly applied during the past century was due to the inability of the Conference to agree upon a convention binding the nations to resort to arbitration in a large number of specified cases. And even in questions of a legal nature, the resort was to be voluntary. That there might, however, be no doubt as to the right of the powers to bind themselves to arbitration, the Conference stated the self-evident in the following language:

" Independently of general or private treaties expressly stipulating recourse to arbitration as obligatory on the Signatory Powers, these powers reserve to themselves the right of concluding, either before the ratification of the present Act or later, new Agreements, general or private, with a view to extending obligatory arbitration to all cases which they may consider it possible to submit to it."

It would seem that the reservation of the right was unnecessary, as sovereign nations, after as well as before the Conference, possessed the right. But it is impossible to read the article without perceiving in its guarded terms a recommendation that such agreements be concluded; and, in fact, this article, useless and superfluous as it may seem to the critical reader, has nevertheless been the starting point of the new movement in favor of treaties of arbitration. With this phase of the subject, however, we are not immediately concerned, and it will not be further considered except to point out the necessity of an agreement between nations either by general or special treaties to carry a case before the court of arbitration.

It may be thought that the Code of Arbitral Procedure applied by the court would properly be considered after the agreement upon the court had been reached. But this is believed to be a narrow view of the case, because a code could be drafted by the Conference with a recommendation that it be used by commissions of arbitration whether or not a code had been devised by the Conference, just in the same way as an expression in favor of arbitration does not necessarily depend upon the creation of the court. But however this may be, it is a fact that the Conference drafted a code of procedure with a view " to encourage the development of arbitration," and that the Signatory Powers agreed upon rules to be applicable to arbitral procedure unless other rules were agreed upon by the parties. (Article 30.)

It will be noted that the code is in the nature of a recommendation, leaving the powers in controversy free to reject its provisions or to modify them according to their pleasure. It is a fact, however, that the recommendation has been, in practice, tantamount to an agreement to apply them, and that the modifications have been trivial. This is another way of saying that the code has been exceedingly valuable and serviceable to the nations at large. As a mixed commission or a special tribunal of the so-called Permanent Court has no jurisdiction except that which is conferred upon it by the parties in dispute, it follows necessarily that an agreement must be reached upon this point. The instrument to do this is technically called the *compromis,* of which the English equivalent is " special agreement " ; and in this, to quote the language of the Convention, " the subject of the difference is clearly defined, as well as the extent of the arbitrators' powers."

The code divides what may be called the pleadings into two parts: one the written pleadings, consisting of the case, the counter-case, and the written arguments; the other the oral arguments before the tribunal in session. It was the intention of the Conference that the printed pleadings should be prepared in advance and served upon the arbitrators before the trial, so that they might familiarize themselves with the case in all its details before the oral proceedings, which consist of the arguments of counsel before the court. As nations are artificial persons, they can only appear by agent and counsel, and therefore agents to conduct the case and counsel to argue it are permitted. Often documents considered to be material to the right understanding and decision of the court have not been furnished to the court. Therefore it is provided that either party may call the tribunal's attention to such documents and request their production, or that the arbitrators themselves may request documents which they regard as material. Again, testimony is taken in national courts and it may be necessary to do so in international tribunals. Therefore a provision is made for the testimony of witnesses, who, however, are not cross-examined by counsel, as in Anglo-American practice, but questioned by the judges, according to the method of the civil law. Finally, a difficult point is often cleared up and doubts removed by questions from the bench. Therefore the judges of the court are authorized to put questions to agents or counsel, with the distinct understanding, however, that such questions are not to be considered as expressing the views of the arbitrators. When the argument is completed and the oral proceedings finished, the judges retire to consider the case and to prepare their award, which is delivered in open court, in the presence of agent or counsel, or in their absence, if they have been duly summoned to appear. The opinion thus rendered adjusts the case, as the *compromis* or special agreement, to quote the language of the Convention, "implies the engagement to submit loyally to the award." There is, unfortunately, in the code no adequate provision for a rehearing, although the right may be reserved in the *compromis* or special agreement " to demand the revision of the award." But, unless this right be reserved, the revision must be made by the tribunal which pronounces the award, and only " on the ground of the discovery of some new fact calculated to exercise a decisive influence on the award and which, at the time the discussion was closed, was unknown to the tribunal and to the party demanding the revision." (Article 55.)

Although it may be admitted that the code was intended primarily for the Court of Arbitration, it is nevertheless true that, based as it is upon the experience of nations with arbitration, it would be applicable to any commission or temporary tribunal, and it is evident that a great service would have been rendered by it to arbitration had the Permanent Court not been established.

We now come to the Permanent Court of Arbitration. It will be recalled that the American delegation was the only one officially instructed to propose such an institution, although it has been stated that the suggestion was in the first instance due to Sir

Julian Pauncefote, at that time British Ambassador at Washington.

The So-Called Permanent Court of Arbitration. It is, therefore, eminently proper that this distinguished statesman and diplomat should receive credit for the proposal, and that he should be considered in a peculiar and personal sense of the word as the father of the court, even although it must be borne in mind that the project was a favorite one with many people in the United States, and that there existed in this country a strong sentiment in favor of its creation.

Without considering in detail the various proposals made at the Conference, it will be sufficient to state and to analyze the ultimate result, so as to make clear the nature of the institution, the rôle which it was expected to play, and the part it actually does play in international relations. But it should be said in this connection that while there was a very general feeling in favor of the court as proposed by Sir Julian Pauncefote, the opposition of the German Government at one time threatened its creation. The reasons, apparently, were two-fold: First, that Germany had not had sufficient experience with arbitration to conclude a general treaty; and, second, that Germany was averse to the establishment of a court which presupposed arbitration treaties and which in the nature of things was likely to be permanent. The scruples of Germany were overcome, in so far as the court was concerned, on condition, however, that a general treaty of arbitration should not be negotiated.

The close connection between arbitration on the one hand and the code of procedure on the other is clearly shown in the introductory article of the section of the Convention for the Pacific Settlement of International Disputes devoted to the Permanent Court, which reads as follows:

"With the object of facilitating an immediate recourse to arbitration for international differences, the Signatory Powers undertake to organize a Permanent Court of Arbitration, accessible at all times and operating, unless otherwise stipulated by the parties, in accordance with the Rules of Procedure inserted in the present Convention." (Article 20.)

The court, however, is one without specific jurisdiction, as the attempt failed to negotiate a general treaty of arbitration binding nations to submit certain classes of disputes. It is also a court without judges, although a list of competent persons is supplied from which the nations can pick and choose the persons desired for the temporary or special tribunal. The court, however, is declared to be competent for all cases of arbitration, reserving to the nations the right to create another and different tribunal. It was to be located in The Hague, and an Administrative Council, consisting of the representatives of the Signatory Powers accredited to The Hague, was to establish the court and an international bureau in connection with it to act as the clerk of the court and to be under the supervision of the Council. The important provisions of the Convention are those relating to the selection of the panel or list of judges, and the formation from this list of the temporary tribunal for the trial and disposition of a case. Other matters will not be considered. The language of the Convention on these points will be quoted without entering into other details which, although interesting, are irrelevant to the matter in hand. Let us first consider the list or panel of judges.

In Article 23 of the Convention it is provided that "each Signatory Power shall select four persons at the most, of known competency in questions of international law, of the highest moral reputation, and disposed to accept the duties of arbitrators." It is provided in a subsequent paragraph of the same article that "two or more powers may agree on the selection in common of one or more members." A list is made of the persons thus selected and the list or panel, as well as any alterations in it, is communicated to the Signatory Powers. The arbitrators are appointed for a term of six years, and may be reappointed for a succeeding period; that is to say, the principle of equality is observed, each state having the privilege of appointing for a period of six years four persons fitted to act as arbitrators and willing to act if appointed, with the result that if each of the 26 states represented at the First Conference avails itself of the right or privilege, there would be a body of 104 persons, and if the 44 powers represented at the Second Hague Conference exercised the right, a body of 176.

The mere statement of these facts without argument shows that we are dealing with a list or panel, or at most with a judicial assembly, not with a court in the strict and technical sense of the word. The Conference, however, was pleased to consider the list or body as a court, and gave it the high-sounding and thoroughly inaccurate name of the " Permanent Court of Arbitration," instead of the more modest but accurate name of the Permanent List or Panel of Arbitrators. It is but natural that delegates should seek to magnify their work; but by using language unjustified by the facts of the case, they have created the impression that a court exists for the trial of cases; that this court is permanent; that it is " accessible at all times," whereas in fact they only created a list or panel of arbiters from which a temporary tribunal could be formed for the trial of a case and which, like a mixed commission, passed out of existence when the award was rendered. It is not denied that their action has called attention to arbitration and the arbitral method of settlement, and given it a prestige and a dignity which it formerly lacked, and that the " hope of facilitating an immediate recourse to arbitration for international differences " was attained. It is believed, however, that the improper use of the terms " court " and " permanent " has made it more difficult to call into being a court in the technical sense of the word, of which permanency is an essential element. Public opinion is not particular about details, and rarely looks below the surface of things. It believes that a court has been established, and argument is required to refute the error and persuasion to have it declare itself in favor of a truly permanent court to be constituted alongside of the so-called Permanent Court, for the judicial decision of legal disputes. It is a fact, however, that public opinion is being enlightened and that, largely through the American Society for Judicial Settlement of International Disputes, the sentiment in the United States in behalf of an international court of justice has been strengthened and created in countries where it did not previously exist.

That the statement is correct that only a list—not a court— was created by the First Conference is evident by Article 24 of the Convention, which provides for the formation of a temporary or special tribunal, to be composed of a number of persons selected by the powers in controversy from the list or panel for the adjustment of the dispute. Much confusion exists in the public mind as to this, and it is within the personal knowledge of the writer that delegates to the Second Hague Conference failed adequately to grasp the distinction between the so-called Permanent Court on the one hand and the temporary or special tribunal on the other. On this very important point, which indeed is fundamental, the Convention says:

" When the Signatory Powers desire to have recourse to the Permanent Court for the settlement of a difference that has arisen between them, the arbitrators called upon to form the competent tribunal to decide this difference must be chosen from the general list of members of the court."   (Article 24.)

That is to say, notwithstanding the use of the term " Permanent Court," the tribunal has to be created for the trial of each particular case. It was foreseen that the nations might agree upon the composition of the Arbitral Tribunal. It was also foreseen that they might not agree, and a method was provided for its composition in the event that the powers either did not or were unable to agree upon its personnel. The following paragraphs from the same article define the method to be used in the latter case:

" Failing the direct agreement of the parties on the composition of the Arbitration Tribunal, the following course shall be pursued:

" Each party appoints two arbitrators, and these together choose an umpire.

" If the votes are equal, the choice of the umpire is intrusted to a third power, selected by the parties by common accord.

" If an agreement is not arrived at on this subject, each party selects a different power, and the choice of the umpire is made in concert by the powers thus selected."

It is to be observed that the special tribunal recommended by the First Hague Conference contemplates a body of five judges, should the parties not otherwise decide, and that of these five judges only one need be a stranger to the dispute, as every nation was authorized to appoint two arbitrators with a presumption in favor of citizens or subjects of their respective countries. The Second Peace Conference, of 1907, greatly improved this provision by providing that only two of the arbiters chosen from the list or panel should be citizens or subjects of the nations in controversy, and added a clause rendering it morally certain that an umpire could be selected, which might not have happened under the original convention.

"Each party appoints two arbitrators, of whom one only can be its national, or chosen from among the persons who have been selected by it as members of the Permanent Court. These arbitrators together choose an umpire.

"If the votes are equally divided, the choice of the umpire is intrusted to a third power, selected by the parties by common accord.

"If an agreement is not arrived at on this subject each party selects a different power, and the choice of the umpire is made in concert by the powers thus selected.

"If, within two months' time, these two powers cannot come to an agreement, each of them presents two candidates taken from the list of members of the Permanent Court, exclusive of the members selected by the parties and not being nationals of either of them. Drawing lots determines which of the candidates thus presented shall be umpire."

(Convention for the Pacific Settlement of International Disputes of 1907, Article 45.)

It is evident, however, that we do not have a permanent court either by the original or revised Convention. We have at most machinery for the creation of a temporary tribunal, and while it is admitted that the machinery created docs as a matter of fact facilitate the recourse to arbitration, it does not remove the greatest difficulty in resorting to it: namely, the composition of a special tribunal at the very time when the parties are not in the frame of mind to form such a tribunal. Without seeking to minimize the importance of either Conference, the writer of this article believes that, were it not for the prestige of a Hague Convention, the situation after the First Conference would have been much the same as it was before: namely, that nations might agree to general or specific treaties of arbitration; that they might constitute temporary tribunals for the settlement of disputes, and that they might use, as they undoubtedly would, the procedure in the form it had assumed during the century which has elapsed since the Jay Treaty.

A dozen tribunals have been formed for the trial of cases at

The Hague, and it is believed that the members of these tribunals would have been much the same had the permanent list or panel not existed. For nations have had a weakness for their subjects or citizens, and they have, wisely it is believed, confined their choice to jurists who derive little or no prestige from being members of the permanent list or panel, but who rather reflect distinction upon it, and who would have been chosen in most cases if the list or panel had not existed. This statement is borne out by an examination of the countries from which judges have been chosen, and by the standing and distinction of the judges themselves. Thus, a well-informed writer says in a recent article:

" In the space of about ten years the Permanent Court of Arbitration settled twelve disputes. France was a party to six of these: America and England, to five; Italy and Germany, to three; Russia and Mexico, Venezuela, Sweden and Norway, each to two; Spain, Belgium, Holland, Turkey and Peru, each to one. In five of the cases Dutch jurists—Asser, de Savornin Lohman and Loeff—acted as judges, and in the first two Dutchmen sat at the same time; Swedish and Norwegian arbitrators—Professor Hammarskjöld and Minister Gram—sat in five of these disputes. France also was represented five times in the arbitration court, Professor Renault being chosen each time. Professor Lammasch, of Austria, who was chosen judge four times, has also rendered very good services; England was represented twice by Sir Edward Fry, once by Sir Charles Fitzpatrick, and once by Lord Desart; Russia twice by Professor de Martens, twice by Baron Taube, and once by Mandelstam, while Fusinato represented Italy in three of the arbitration courts. The prominent place that Holland occupies with Sweden in this list is the more remarkable, if it is borne in mind that it has never submitted a case to the Permanent Court, and thus has never appointed a judge."

Effect of Hague Conference on Arbitration. It should be said, however, that the action of the Hague Conference in recognizing arbitration and creating machinery to resort to it has called it to the attention of the world in a way which would not otherwise have been possible, and that, however imperfect the machinery may be, the action of the Conferences has given a greater impetus to arbitration than any act of recorded history. It is, nevertheless, childish to regard the work of the Conference as perfect or final, and to resent any and every amendment because it seems to question the efficiency or finality of the conventions of the two Conferences. Those who propose amendments to render the machinery more effective in the future than in the past are, it is believed, the true friends of progress and, therefore, of the Conferences. Taking their work as a starting-point and modifying and developing it to meet the changing needs of nations would tend to make the Conference a living and a vital force for the future rather than considering their work as done and final. For by so doing we minimize their importance as international agencies and we confine within narrow limits the scope of their activities.

Distinction Between Arbitration and Judicial Settlement Fundamental. If, however, we consider the institution created by the First Conference and modified in certain important details by the Second as in reality a court, it is nevertheless, according to its name, a court of arbitration. And if we suppose that it adequately meets the needs of arbitration, the question arises whether or not arbitration as understood and practised is the ultimate goal toward which we tend, or whether arbitration is but a step toward judicial settlement. But before discussing this interesting question, we should determine whether arbitration and judicial settlement are synonymous, or whether in fact, if not in theory, they differ in essential particulars. For if arbitration and judicial settlement be identical, it necessarily follows that a movement in favor of judicial settlement as distinguished from arbitration is without reason; whereas if the two methods differ, arbitration may be preferred in some cases and judicial settlement in others, so that these methods of peaceful settlement will co-exist and mutually aid one another, or arbitration may merge in judicial settlement. The writer believes that in fact, if not in theory, these two systems differ, not merely in form, but in substance; that certain classes of disputes should be and can only be decided by judicial process; that the failure to recognize the distinction and to provide machinery for its exercise retards the movement in favor of international peace. He admits, however, that certain questions can be better adjusted by arbitration than decided by courts of justice, and that there is, therefore, every prospect that arbitration would still be resorted to, even although an international court of justice were created for the decision of cases by judicial process.

The object of international arbitration is declared to be " the settlement of differences between states by judges of their own choice, and on the basis of respect for law." The object of judicial decision, on the contrary, is the decision of differences by judges, not necessarily chosen by the parties in controversy, by an application of principles of law, not on the basis of respect for law.

The difference between the purposes of each is believed to be fundamental, and a failure to grasp the difference leads to erroneous and unjustifiable conclusions. Arbiters of the parties' own choice are not necessarily impartial, and, if they were not supposed to be friendly to the litigants, or at least open to argument by them, they would not be chosen. Judges are not selected by the parties and, being strangers to the dispute, are presumed to be impartial, for there is no necessary relation between their choice and their decision. They do not owe their appointment to the litigants, and they neither do nor can receive reward from them. The umpire, it may be admitted, is an indifferent person, but he is not independent. He is subject to the argument and influence of his national, and therefore biased, associates, and his future selection as umpire depends upon the satisfaction which he may have given to the litigants in a particular case. The revised method of selecting the tribunal, devised by the Second Hague Conference, secures or may secure three indifferent persons instead of one, and it may thus be said that the adjustment of the case is reached by a tribunal composed of a majority of indifferent persons. But this distinction is more specious than real, because after, as before the Conference the parties compose the tribunal according to their pleasure, and if they adopt the method proposed by the Second Conference and select the arbitrators from the permanent list or panel, they may choose one citizen or subject, and another person who, although a foreigner, nevertheless may be considered as friendly to the contention; otherwise he would not be chosen. We, therefore, have two citizens or biased subjects, two friends, and an indifferent umpire, whose future choice as umpire, or indeed as arbitrator in a different case, depends upon the satisfaction which he has given to one or the other of the contending parties. It needs no argument to show that judges are not exposed to such criticism.

In the next place, it is believed that a settlement " on the basis of respect for law " may be an adjustment or a judicial decision, according to the amount of respect which the arbiters may be pleased to give to law. It is not necessarily a judicial decision, as in the case of judges bound to administer and to apply law. It makes no difference whether the judge respects law or has no liking for it; if it exists, he applies it. His action is impersonal; or, to use a continental expression, his action is objective—not subjective—for the personal element has been eliminated. The element of uncertainty, therefore, exists in arbitration, which is excluded in judicial decision, although judges, as human beings, may be mistaken either as to the existence of a principle of law or as to its application. So may arbiters if they sit and act as judges; but the mistake of the judge may be corrected on appeal, whereas an appeal is inconsistent with the object of arbitration, which contemplates " a settlement " of the controversy and an appeal is contrary to the express wording of the convention, which, according to Article 18, " implies the engagement to submit loyally to the award."

But there is, it is believed, another point of view from which the subject may be approached, which leads inevitably to the same conclusion. Arbitration is, by Article 20, to settle differences " which it has not been possible to settle by diplomacy "; that is to say, arbitration springs out of diplomacy, or takes up the question where diplomacy has left it, and it is feared that the spirit of compromise inherent in diplomatic adjustments is carried over into arbitral procedure and finds no inconspicuous place in the award. Indeed, in the one country, Switzerland, which for centuries settled disputes between its cantons by arbitration the arbiters chosen by the parties acted as mediators and offered a settlement or an adjustment which, if accepted, settled the dispute. Upon its rejection, they took up the cause anew, and, to use the language of the Hague Conference, adjusted it " on the basis of respect for law." It is very difficult for one man to have two functions, and to draw a clean-cut line of distinction between their exercise. The executive, the legislative, and the judicial powers are separated in constitutional countries, and it is believed that the experience of nations should not be lost upon arbitrators. It should be clearly known that they act either as diplomats and reach a compromise, as is proper in case of diplomatic adjustment, or that they are judges and reach a judicial decision, as becomes judges. Until this is done, uncertainty exists, and uncertainty, it is submitted, either will or should prevent a resort to that form of procedure from which it is not excluded. Competent critics have examined the awards of the Hague tribunals and have pointed out the presence of compromise as distinguished from judicial decision, and their criticism is the more damaging as they are believed to be partisans of arbitration rather than outspoken advocates of judicial decision. It is reported by the faithful Boswell that Lord Mansfield once advised Dr. Johnson to believe one-half of what a certain person said, to which Dr. Johnson replied: "Ay, but we don't know which half to believe." Where compromise is possible and found to exist, we naturally, like Dr. Johnson, question the entire award.

Now, if it be said that judicial decision is open to the charge of uncertainty, we may, as is the custom with lawyers, confess and avoid. That is to say, we may confess that neither the litigants nor the lawyers can predict with certainty the outcome of the case any more than the same persons could predict the arbitral award, but we avoid the consequences of the admission in the case of judicial decision by stating that if we cannot absolutely forecast the judgment, we can, nevertheless, predict it within certain clearly defined limits. For instance, if the plaintiff insists upon the existence of a certain fact or of a principle of law as decisive of his case, and if the defendant denies the existence of the fact or the principle of law which governs it, and suggests a different principle of law as applicable, it is evident that finding the fact to exist or not to exist, or the non-existence or the non-applicability of the principle of law decides the case. The client and the lawyer may thus predict in the alternative the inevitable results.

This is not the case with diplomats who frankly compromise. It is not the case with arbiters who may compromise. It is the case with judges who must find the fact, declare the fact to be as it is found, and who must apply the principle of law contended for by plaintiff or defendant, if such principle of law exist. In the case of diplomats, the governments control their action, for they are the agents of their own choice and the governments determine with a fullness of knowledge what they are willing or unwilling to compromise.   In case of arbiters, nations cannot directly control the award, although they may have taken every precaution to choose persons favorable to their respective contentions; for, although the arbiters are appointed by them, they are not, as diplomatic agents, subjected to their direct control.   The compromise cannot be foreseen, if it is to be a compromise, and they cannot determine in advance whether the award will be acceptable, although they have bound themselves " to submit loyally to the award," to quote the exact language of the convention.

If, therefore, the feeling becomes prevalent, as it promises to become, that arbitration is either a thing of compromise or may be such, according to the arbiters' respect for law, it would seem to follow that nations would prefer agents whom they can control rather than arbiters whose award may be a compromise which they would not have authorized in advance.   Nevertheless, they may be willing to submit their legal questions to judicial decision, because they can predict the outcome in the alternative, knowing what they may expect and making in advance the arrangements necessary to comply with the judgment.   There will, however—at least the present writer so believes—always be large issues of a more or less political nature, which nations can only expect to have settled on the principle of give and take, and when direct negotiations have failed, they may properly resort and, indeed, be willing to resort to compromisers of their own choice, because in the larger point of view it is better to have these controversies out of the way, even although certain contentions be renounced, than to have them embitter their foreign relations, as they will assuredly do unless settled.   But just as large oaks from little acorns grow, so great questions of policy which are mere matters of law in the beginning become by delay and mismanagement political questions upon which nations are willing to stake their existence and the lives of their inhabitants.   If, however, a permanent court of justice existed, to which these legal matters could be referred automatically when and as they arise, and before the nations have taken position upon them and public opinion has expressed itself, they might be got out of the way so quietly as to pass unnoticed except to the foreign offices which rejoice at their settlement, and the experts in international law whose business it is to study such matters.

An International Court of Justice a Necessary Complement to Arbitration.

It is not because the partisans of judicial decision believe the decision of a court will settle all questions, or that it is fitted to decide political questions, that they advocate its establishment. They know by experience that courts of law only pass upon legal questions, and that the thousand and one questions of policy which trouble and perplex men of affairs neither find their way into court nor are fitted for judicial decision. However large the jurisdiction of a court may be, it is nevertheless a limited jurisdiction and does not include questions of policy or of preference. And the partisans of judicial settlement believe that an international court of justice will, in the nature of things, if established, be a court of limited jurisdiction. They feel, however, that a judicial tribunal will be an additional guaranty of peace between nations, and that without supplanting any agency, it will do either what other agencies cannot do, or do but imperfectly. Their hope is to enlarge and yet confine the peace movement by basing it upon the solid foundation of law and justice, and by providing adequate agencies for their application. They believe that there is a fundamental distinction between the nature and the result of arbitration on the one hand and the nature and the result of judicial decision on the other, and impressed by this distinction and its importance, they have advocated and still do advocate the introduction of judicial procedure into the practice of nations and the creation of a permanent tribunal composed of judges by profession, acting according to judicial standards. Fortunately, this conception of what the writer ventures to call the new order of things found a spokesman in the person of Mr. Elihu Root, who, as Secretary of State, instructed the American delegates to the Second Conference to propose such a tribunal. The passage of his instructions is so short and to the point that it is equally difficult to abridge or to add to it. Like the acorn, it has the giant oak within. It is, therefore, quoted in full:

" The method in which arbitration can be made more effective, so that nations may be more ready to have recourse to it voluntarily and to enter into treaties by which they bind themselves to submit to it, is indicated by observation of the weakness of the system now apparent. There can be no doubt that the principal objection to arbitration rests not upon the unwillingness of nations to submit their controversies to impartial arbitration, but upon an apprehension that the arbitrations to which they submit may not be impartial.

"It has been a very general practice for arbitrators to act, not as judges deciding questions of fact and law upon the record before them under a sense of judicial responsibility, but as negotiators affecting settlements of the questions brought before them in accordance with the traditions and usages and subject to all the considerations and influences which affect diplomatic agents. The two methods are radically different, proceed upon different standards of honorable obligation, and frequently lead to widely differing results. It very frequently happens that a nation which would be very willing to submit its differences to an impartial judicial determination is unwilling to subject them to this kind of diplomatic process.

"If there could be a tribunal which would pass upon questions between nations with the same impartial and impersonal judgment that the Supreme Court of the United States gives to questions arising between citizens of the different states, or between foreign citizens and the citizens of the United States, there can be no doubt that nations would be much more ready to submit their controversies to its decision than they are now to take the chances of arbitration.

"It should be your effort to bring about in the Second Conference a development of the Hague Tribunal into a permanent tribunal composed of judges who are judicial officers and nothing else, who are paid adequate salaries, who have no other occupation, and who will devote their entire time to the trial and decision of international causes by judicial methods and under a sense of judicial responsibility. These judges should be so selected from the different countries that the different systems of law and procedure and the principal languages shall be fairly represented. The court should be made of such dignity, consideration and rank that the

best and ablest jurists will accept appointment to it, and that the
whole world will have absolute confidence in its judgments."

Accordingly, acting under these instructions, the American delegation submitted a project (printed in the appendix) for the establishment of a court in the sense in which that term is used by
jurists.

**The Project
of the American
Delegates.**
The project is stated in general terms and
was only intended to serve as a basis of discussion, not to be adopted in the form submitted. It contemplated a court to be composed of fifteen judges without determining
the manner of their appointment, but provided that the different
countries and the systems of law and procedure, as well as the principal languages, should be represented; that the court should meet
annually at The Hague and should remain in session until the business before it was transacted; that as a court it should draw up
its regulations; that as a court, national judges should be excluded,
except upon the express consent of the parties; that without original
jurisdiction, it should be competent to decide all differences of an
international character between nations which diplomacy had failed
to settle and which the parties in controversy agreed to submit to
the court; that it should serve as a court of appeal for the findings,
decisions, awards of commissions of inquiry, and all special tribunals of arbitration which might be submitted by the respective
parties thereto; and that the judges of the proposed court should
be competent to act as members of commissions of inquiry or as
special tribunals, should the nations desire them so to act. It
should be noted also that the proposed court was not intended to
replace the so-called permanent court, for by Article 6 it was expressly stated that this latter institution " might, as far as possible,
constitute the basis " of the proposed court, with the distinct pro-
viso, however, that the nations excluded from the First Conference,
but which participated in the Second, should be represented in it.
The difference between the actual so-called Permanent Court of
Arbitration and the projected court is, it is believed, the difference
between a mixed commission and a technical court, and the determination of the advocates of the latter to regularize and to in-
ternationalize the practice of nations is evident from the fact that

the court was to sit as a court of appeal for review or revision of decisions of an international nature, no matter by what agency they might have been rendered. The American delegation drafted and was prepared to lay before the Conference a project of nineteen articles, giving effect to Mr. Root's instructions, based upon the brief 'statement of the elements which should enter into the constitution and operation of such a court, as outlined in the project previously submitted, which has been sufficiently analyzed for present purposes.

Germany and Great Britain. The desire of Germany and Great Britain to present a joint project caused the American delegation to withhold its original draft, which, however, is printed in the appendix in order to enable the reader the better to comprehend the proposal of the three countries, loyally supported by France, although it was not technically a party. After weeks of discussion, a project of thirty-five articles was approved by the Conference, voted by it on October 16, 1907, although it is imperfect in the sense that it does not prescribe the method by which the judges were to be appointed. This was not merely a difficulty; it was fatal to the establishment of the court, because a court without judges is inoperative, if not unthinkable. But the matter did not rest here, for, as has been stated, the Conference adopted the project and recommended that the tribunal be established when the nations should agree upon a method of appointing the judges. The labor, therefore, was not in vain. It is competent for any number of nations to install the court for themselves, and if this be done we shall have a court of justice between nations just as we have a supreme judicial tribunal in every State that makes a pretense to civilization.

The Main Features of the Proposed International Court. What are the main features of the proposed permanent court of justice? It is believed that the official account of the court as contained in the official report of the American delegation to the Secretary of State should properly be quoted, as it shows the sense in which it was understood and interpreted by the delegation, and it is the court as interpreted and explained by the delegation which the United States has tried through diplomatic channels to establish.

" ' The Conference recommends to the Signatory Powers the adoption of the project hereunto annexed, of a convention for the establishment of a court of arbitral justice and its putting in effect as soon as an accord shall be reached upon the choice of the judges and the constitution of the court.' "

" An analysis of this paragraph shows that the establishment of the court is not the expression of a mere wish or desire on the part of the Conference, but that it is a recommendation to the powers to undertake the establishment of the court. In the next place, the project of convention annexed to the recommendation is not to be submitted as a plan or as a model, but for adoption as the organic act of the court. Again, the convention annexed and made a part of the recommendation goes forth not only with the approval of the Conference but as a solemn act adopted by it. And, finally, accepting the convention as the organic act, the Conference recommends that the court be definitely and permanently established by the powers as soon as they shall have agreed upon a method of appointing the judges, who, when appointed, thus constitute the court. It will be noted that the number of powers necessary to establish the court is not stated, nor is the number of judges determined. It follows, therefore, that the powers wishing to establish the court are free to adopt the project of convention, agree upon the method of choosing the judges, and establish the court at The Hague for the trial of cases submitted by the contracting powers.

" The establishment of the court of arbitral justice would not interfere with the court of arbitration instituted by the Conference of 1899 and continued by the Conference of 1907, for this latter is a temporary tribunal, erected for a particular purpose, to decide as arbiters a controversy submitted. The court of arbitral justice, on the contrary, is meant to be a permanent court, composed of judges acting under a sense of judicial responsibility, representing the various legal systems of the world, and capable of assuring the continuity of arbitral jurisprudence (Article 1). The contracting powers are free to appoint either a large or a small number of judges; but it is provided in Article 3 that the judges so appointed shall hold office for a period of twelve years, and that they shall be chosen from among persons enjoying the highest moral consideration, who meet the requirements for admission in their respective countries to the high magistracy, or who shall be jurists of recognized competency in matters of international law (Article 2).

" From these provisions it is evident that the proposed institution is to be not merely in name but in fact a court of justice; that it is to be permanent in the sense that it does not need to be constituted for any and every case submitted to it. It is obvious that such a court, acting under a sense of judicial responsibility, would decide, as a court, according to international law and equity, a question submitted to it, and that the idea of compromise hitherto so inseparable from arbitration, would be a stranger to this institution. The court is said to be permanent in the sense that it holds, as courts do, certain specified terms for the trial of cases. For example, Article 14 says:

" The court assembles in session once a year. The session begins on the third Wednesday of June and lasts until the calendar shall have been exhausted.

" The court does not assemble in session if the meeting is deemed unnecessary by the delegation. If, however, a power is a party to a case actually pending before the court, the preliminary proceedings of which are completed or near completion, that power has the right to demand that the session take place.

" The delegation may, in case of necessity, call an extraordinary session of the court."

" It was deemed inexpedient to have an empty court at The Hague, and it was felt that without a judicial committee capable of transacting the ordinary business that might be submitted permanency in the true sense of the word would be lacking, therefore it is provided by Article 6 of the project that:

" The Court designates, every year, three judges who constitute a special delegation and three others who are to take their places in case of disability. They may be re-elected. The vote is cast by blanket ballot. Those who obtain the larger number of votes are considered to be elected. The delegation elects its own president, who, failing a majority, is drawn by lot.

" A member of the delegation is barred ·from the exercise of his functions when the power by which he was appointed and under whose jurisdiction he is one of the parties to the case.

" The members of the delegation bring to a conclusion the cases that may have been referred to therein, even though their term of office should have expired."

" Taking the two articles together, it is apparent that the court as such is intended to be permanently in session at The Hague; that the judicial committee will attend to the smaller cases submitted, and that the full court will meet in ordinary or extraordinary session once a year or whenever the business before it would justify its assembling. The judges are intended to be permanent court officials and as such to receive stated salaries whether they are actively engaged at The Hague in the trial of cases or not. The compensation is small (six thousand florins), but the honor is great. If, however, a judge sits as a trial judge at The Hague, his expenses to and from The Hague are paid according to the rate allowed in the home country for the travelling expenses of a judge in service, and in addition the judge is to receive the further sum of one hundred florins a day during his official service in the examination or trial of cases.

" The first article speaks of a court free and easy of access. It is easy of access because it is permanent and has stated terms. It is free because no fees are paid for entrance, and it is likewise free in this sense: That the salaries of the judges are not paid by the litigating parties, but proportionately by the contracting powers. The jurisdiction of the court is very wide; for example, " the court of arbitral justice is competent to decide all cases which are submitted to it by virtue of a general stipulation of arbitration or by a special agreement " (Article 17) ; that is to say, if there be a general treaty of arbitration designating the court of arbitral justice, the court is competent, if the cause of action be presented, to assume jurisdiction and to decide the case. It may be that parties to a controversy may submit the findings of a commission of inquiry to the court in order to have the legal responsibility established in an appropriate case, or it may be that parties to an arbitration may wish to have the case examined when on appeal or *de novo* by the court of arbitral justice. In such a case, by virtue of the special agreement of the parties litigant, the court is invested with jurisdiction.

" It was not thought advisable to clothe the judicial committee with the jurisdiction of the full court, lest there be two competing institutions. The judicial committee is, however, expected to be a serviceable body, and its jurisdiction is commensurate with its dignity. For example, Article 18 provides:

"'The delegation (Article 6) is competent:

"'1. To hear arbitration cases coming under the foregoing article, if the parties agree upon demanding the application of summary procedure as determined in Title IV, Ch. IV, of the Convention of July 29, 1899.

"'2. To institute an inquiry by virtue of and in conformity to Title III of the Convention of July 29, 1899, in so far as the delegation may have been charged with this duty by the litigants acting in common accord. With the assent of the parties and in derogation of Article 7, Section 1, members of the delegation who took part in the inquiry may sit as judges if the dispute comes for arbitration before either the court or the delegation itself.'

"The judicial committee, therefore, is competent to sit as the court of summary proceeding in cases where parties litigant agree to make use of the summary proceeding of the revised convention. It is likewise competent to sit as a commission of inquiry; and as the commission of inquiry finds facts, there seems to be no reason why the members of the judicial committee may not sit as judges if the litigation is submitted to the full court or to the delegation.

"Article 19 invests the judicial committee with the power to frame the special agreement—that is to say, the *compromis* provided for in Article 52 of the convention for the peaceful adjustment of international differences, already mentioned—unless there be an agreement or stipulation to the contrary.

"The procedure of the court has not been neglected, but finds an appropriate place in the project of convention.

"The establishment of the Permanent Court was proposed by the American delegation, was accepted in principle and loyally supported by the delegations of Germany and Great Britain, and the project actually framed and recommended by the Conference is the joint work of the American, German and British delegations. It should be said, however, that the project could not have been adopted without the loyal and unstinted support of France.

"From this brief exposition it is evident that the foundations of a Permanent Court have been broadly and firmly laid; that the organization, jurisdiction and procedure have been drafted and rec-ommended in the form of a code which the powers or any number of them may accept and, by agreeing upon the appointment of judges, call into being a court at once permanent and international. A little time, a little patience, and the great work is accomplished."

It would have been well to retain, in the project as adopted by the Conference, Article 13 of the original draft as prepared but not submitted by the American delegation. Had this been done we would have had a court of justice competent to decide every dis-pute of an international nature submitted to it, and the invitation to appear before it and to submit to its jurisdiction would have been in fact, if not in theory, tantamount to the summons of na-tional courts. This article, however, was not retained. It is im-portant, and the services it would render have been pointed out by the distinguished Professor Nys, who is not only an international lawyer of the highest standing, intent upon the equality and sover-eignty of states which he would not wish to see violated, but who sees in the administration of justice by an international tribunal composed of judges the realization of international peace. As a judge he recognizes the limitations as well as the advantages of ju-dicial process.

In an interesting article contributed to the *American Journal of International Law* (Vol. 6, pp. 308-10) Professor Nys says:

" An ingenious proposal [Article 13 of the American draft] was submitted to various members of the Second Hague Confer-ence regarding the jurisdiction of the permanent judicial court which was to be established. According to this plan the court shall be competent to receive, consider and determine any claims or pe-titions from a sovereign state touching any difference of an inter-national character with another sovereign State, provided that such difference is not political in character and does not involve the honor, independence and vital interests of any state. It shall not be competent concerning any petition or application from any per-son, natural or artificial, except a sovereign state. It shall not take any action on any petition or application which it is competent to receive, unless it shall be of the opinion that a justiciable case, and one which it is competent to entertain and decide and worthy of its consideration, has been brought before it, in which case it may, in not less than thirty nor more than ninety days after the presentation of the petition, invite the other sovereign state to appear and submit the matter to judicial determination by the court. It follows that it would be possible for a state to call another state to the bar and thus bring about a judicial presentation of the question. It is true that one danger exists which must be avoided—that of wounding the pride of a sovereign state. However, the following provision obviates the difficulty: Should the court invite a state to appear and submit the matter to judicial determination, the state so invited may (a) refuse to submit the matter; (b) refrain from submitting the matter by failing for a certain number of days to make any response to the invitation, in which event it shall be deemed to have refused; (c) submit the matter in whole; (d) offer to submit the matter in part or in different form from that stated in the petition, in which event the petitioning state shall be free either to accept the qualified submission or to withdraw its petition or application; (e) appear for the sole purpose of denying the right of the petitioning state to any redress or relief; in case the court does not sustain this, it shall renew the invitation to appear. In case the states in controversy cannot agree upon the form and scope of the submission of the difference referred to in the petition, the court may appoint, upon the request of either party, a committee of three from the Administrative Council, and this committee shall frame the questions to be submitted and the scope of the inquiry, and thereafter if either party shall withdraw, it shall be deemed to have refused to submit the matter involved to judicial determination. If such a procedure could be decided upon, all the difficulties which beset the path of arbitration would be overcome. The court of justice would be ready to hear the lawyers and representatives of the states, parties to the cause, and it could act in its capacity as a judicial tribunal and arbitration would be superfluous. There would be no longer necessity for general arbitration conventions, nor special *compromis* concluded with regard to a particular dispute; all states would be in the presence of a true international tribunal and in the position of the citizen of a civilized country who, having an injury done to his rights, may cité him whom he accuses to have been the author of the wrong to meet him before established tribunals."

Why the Court
Was Not Actually
Established at
the Second Hague
Conference.

If it be asked why the Conference approved in principle the establishment of an international court, badly named "the Court of Arbitral Justice," and yet failed to constitute the court by the appointment of judges, the answer is that no delegation other than that of the United States was instructed to propose the formation of such a court; that the question was difficult in view of the conflicting desire of the large and of the small nations to be represented in it; that the time at the disposal of the Conference was limited, being in session but four months in all, and that many and important subjects had to be considered. The larger nations wished permanent representation. The smaller nations likewise wished to be represented. If each nation could have appointed a judge, it would have been easy to compose the court, but we should then have had a judicial assembly of forty-four members, as forty-four states were represented at the Conference, not a court of a limited number. From this point of view the difficulty was mathematical, and no satisfactory method was found at the time to reduce forty-four to fifteen without excluding judges from some of the states. A compromise was contemplated, for it would have been possible for the convention to recommend the appointment of certain persons peculiarly qualified to form the court in the first instance, and to choose their successors through diplomatic channels, or by methods to be determined later. The judges, however, were to be appointed by nations, and naturally the smaller nations were unwilling to admit that their interests in such a court were less than the interests of the larger powers, or that their influence in the constitution of the court should be less as a matter of right, although it might be so as a matter of fact. It would have been better to have discarded the national element entirely and to have selected the judges with reference to their fitness without making their appointment depend upon the representation of certain nations, although the nations naturally would have to decide the question of fitness. The American delegation was willing to accept any method which would produce an adequate court, whether or not a citizen of the United States should be chosen, a statement specifically made by the delegation in the discussion of the matter. Other nations, however, refused to do this. It should be said that Mr. Choate, on behalf of the American delegation, laid before the Conference ten different and distinct methods of composing the court, in an address which is included in the appendix, and it is believed that no more practical methods have been since proposed. It is deeply to be regretted that the court was not created at the Conference, but it is only a fable that Minerva sprang fully equipped from the head of Jove. The acceptance of the principle carries with it its consequences, and sooner or later—its partisans hope it may be soon—the principle is bound to be put into practice and an international court of justice established between nations.

Another reason why the court was not created was, to use an expression of daily occurrence at the Conference, that the time was not ripe for it. This, it is to be feared, is a polite excuse for failing to do what one does not want to do, and yet it is a fact that however strongly public sentiment in the United States may have wished the court, it cannot be said that public opinion existed in its favor in other countries. But public sentiment grows with time. The servants of the people, not excluding therefrom delegates of international conferences, lend a willing ear to its dictation, and public sentiment has declared itself in favor of the court since the adjournment of the Conference.

The recommendation of the Conference that the international court be established through diplomatic channels after the adjournment was not meant to be a dead letter, and the sponsors have not regarded it as tantamount to a decent burial of the proposition, for each of the interested powers, including France, has stated its willingness, and indeed its intention, to co-operate in its constitution, not only by word of mouth at the Conference, but in formal and official statements. Let us examine these official statements in alphabetical order of the names of the countries in French, as is the wont of diplomacy.

In the official report on the Conference, known as the White Book, laid before the Reichstag, the German Government said:

"The organization of such an arbitral court was proposed at the Conference by the United States of America. The proposal sought, as far as possible, to facilitate arbitration, and for that pur-

pose to create a permanent universal court of justice composed
in a definite manner, which should meet each year
at The Hague, in order to decide, free of cost, all
controversies submitted to it by the contracting
powers.   Such an organization appeared to be a
thoroughly appropriate step, which met also the purposes which Germany sought to attain.   The German
delegation, therefore, earnestly supported the proposal, and in co-
operation with the American and British delegation drafted and
submitted an adequate proposition to the Conference.   The proposal
did not, however, lead to the conclusion of a treaty, for the reason
that the members of the Conference recommended the powers to
accept the draft based upon the proposal referred to, as soon as
an agreement could be reached in regard to an appropriate composition of the court.   Germany stands ready to *co-operate* in the
establishment of the court."

Attitude of Powers Proposing the Court.

In the French report, known as the Yellow Book, it is said:

" Each of the states must exert special efforts to carry out, as
far as possible, the *voeux,* resolutions or recommendations, by
which the Conference, in matters upon which it could not reach a
conclusion, has emphatically signified its desire to see the governments complete its work.   It will suffice to refer to the negotiations
requisite to give definitive form to the permanent Court of Arbitral
Justice, whose operation depends upon an agreement regarding the
manner of selecting the judges."

The British Blue Book, after regretting the failure of the Conference to create a court, expressed the hope that it may be instituted, saying:

" We cannot but hope that the difficulties which we have
been unable to overcome may in the end be surmounted,
and that our labor as pioneers may in the end not prove entirely
fruitless."

The American report, already quoted, says on this point:

" It is evident that the foundations of a Permanent Court have
been broadly and firmly laid; that the organization, jurisdiction and
procedure have been drafted and recommended in the form of a
code which the powers, or any number of them, may accept, and
by agreeing upon the appointment of judges, call into being a court

at once permanent and international.   A little time, a little patience, and the great work is accomplished."

This latter statement should be supplemented by a passage from the President's Message to Congress of December, 1907:

" Substantial progress was also made towards the creation of a permanent judicial tribunal for the determination of international causes.   There was very full discussion of the proposal for such a court and a general agreement was finally reached in favor of its creation.   The Conference recommended to the Signatory Powers the adoption of a draft upon which it agreed for the organization of the court, leaving to be determined only the method by which the judges would be selected.   This remaining unsettled question is plainly one which time and good temper will solve."

Efforts to Establish the Court Since the Second Hague Conference.
It thus appears that each of the interested governments has confirmed the action of its delegates at the Conference and that each stands ready to co-operate in the establishment of the court.   It is well known that steps have been taken, as recommended by the Conference, to establish the court and that, as was eminently proper, the American Government took the initiative.   It is difficult to state what has been done, as diplomatic notes are not ordinarily made public during negotiations, and it would probably be regarded as a breach of confidence by the governments chiefly concerned if the notes were published at this time.   An official note of the Department of State has, however, been published, giving some interesting information as to the action of the United States. From this source it is learned that Mr. Robert Bacon, as Secretary of State, took advantage of the meeting of the Naval Conference at London in 1908-9 to propose that the International Prize Court should be invested with the jurisdiction and functions of the Court of Arbitral Justice, and that when so sitting it should act in accordance with the draft convention for the establishment of the arbitral court, adopted by the Conference and recommended to the powers.   Mr. Bacon's instruction was dated February 6, 1909, and is as follows:

" In order to confer upon the Prize Court the functions of an arbitral court contemplated in the first recommendation of the final act of the Second Conference, the Department proposes the following article additional to the draft protocol concerning the Prize Court, next to the last paragraph of your instructions:

" 'And any signatory of the convention for the establishment of the Prize Court may provide further in the act of ratification thereof that the international court of prize shall be competent to accept jurisdiction of and decide any case arising between signatories of this proposed article submitted to it for arbitration, and the International Prize Court shall thereupon accept jurisdiction and adopt for its consideration and decision of the case the project of convention for the establishment of a Court of Arbitral Justice adopted by the Second Hague Conference, the establishment of which was recommended by the powers through diplomatic channels.

" 'Any signatory of the convention for the establishment of the international court of prize may include in its ratification thereof the proposed articles and become entitled to the benefits thereof.'

" The Department earnestly hopes and urges adoption of the proposed articles."

The Naval Conference considered the proposal to invest the Prize Court with the jurisdiction and functions of the Court of Arbitral Justice as beyond its scope, and suggested that a matter of such magnitude should be prosecuted through diplomatic channels. Therefore, on March 5, 1909, Secretary Bacon notified the countries represented at the Maritime Conference of the intention of the United States to prepare and to transmit an identic circular note showing

" The advisability of investing the Prize Court with the jurisdiction and functions of a court of arbitral justice in order that international law may be administered and justice done in peace as well as in war by a permanent international tribunal; that this close connection between the two courts was contemplated by the framers of the arbitral court as appears from Article 16 of the draft convention by virtue of which the judges of the arbitral court might exercise the functions of judges in the Prize Court. The failure to constitute the arbitral court, although the method of appointing judges was substantially the same for both courts, renders this provision ineffective, but it is possible to carry out the intent of the proposers in this and to constitute the arbitral court by investing the Prize Court with the functions of an arbitral court and to prescribe the draft convention of the arbitral court as a code of procedure when so acting."

It is important to quote another passage from Mr. Bacon's instruction of March 5, 1909, as it shows not only the earnest desire of the Government, but that the consent of the powers to the establishment of the court should depend solely upon their matured judgment:

"It is not the intention of this Government to use pressure of any kind to secure the acceptance of its views, but the United States feels that the constitution of the Arbitral Court as a branch or chamber of the Prize Court for the nations voluntarily consenting thereto would not only enhance the dignity of the Prize Court, but by creating a permanent court of arbitration would contribute in the greatest manner to the cause of judicial, and therefore peaceable, settlement of international difficulties."

Mr. Bacon's successor, Mr. Philander C. Knox, therefore made the formal proposition, in a note dated October 18, 1909, from which the following passages are quoted:

"It has been a subject of profound regret to the Government and people of the United States that a Court of Arbitral Justice, composed of permanent judges and acting under a sense of judicial responsibility, representing the various judicial systems of the world and capable of insuring continuity in arbitral jurisprudence, was not established at the Second Hague Peace Conference, and the United States likewise regrets that the composition of the proposed Court of Arbitral Justice has not yet been effected through diplomatic channels, in accordance with the following recommendation of the Conference:

"'The Conference recommends to the Signatory Powers the adoption of the project, hereunto annexed, of a convention for the establishment of a court of arbitral justice and its putting into effect as soon as an agreement shall have been reached as to the choice of the judges and the constitution of the court.'

"A careful consideration of the project and of the difficulties preventing the constitution of the court, owing to the shortness of time at the disposal of the Conference, has led the Government of the United States to the conclusion that it is necessary in the interest of arbitration and the peaceful settlement of international disputes to take up the question of the establishment of the court as recommended by the recent Conference at The Hague and secure through diplomatic channels its institution.

" The necessary and close connection between the International Prize Court and the proposed Court of Arbitral Justice was indicated in Article 16 of the draft convention of the Court of Arbitral Justice, as follows:

" ' The judges and deputy judges, members of the Judicial Arbitration Court, can also exercise the functions of judge and deputy judge in the International Prize Court.'

" The reason which existed in 1907 and led to the formulation of the articles still continues. It has, therefore, occurred to the United States that the difficulty in the way of reaching an agreement upon the composition of the court would be obviated by giving practical effect to Article 16 by an international agreement by virtue of which the judges of the International Prize Court should be competent to sit as judges of the Court of Arbitral Justice for such nations as may freely consent thereto, and that when so sitting the judges of the International Prize Court shall entertain jurisdiction of any case of arbitration submitted by a signatory for their determination and decide the same in accordance with the procedure prescribed in the draft convention. In proposing to invest the International Prize Court with the jurisdiction and functions of the proposed Court of Arbitral Justice the United States is actuated by the desire to establish a court of arbitration permanently in session at The Hague for the peaceful solution of controversies arising in time of peace between the nations accepting and applying in their foreign relations the principles of an enlightened and progressive law.

" It is a truism that it is easier to enlarge the jurisdiction of an existing institution than to call a new one into being, and as the judges and deputy judges of the International Prize Court must be thoroughly versed in international law and of the highest moral reputation, there can be no logical or inherent objection to enlarging their sphere of beneficent influence in vesting them with the quality of judges of the proposed Court of Arbitral Justice.

"The proposal of the United States does not involve the modification either of the letter or spirit of the draft convention, nor would it require a change in wording of any of its articles. It would, however, secure the establishment of the Court of Arbitral Justice as a chamber of the world's first international judiciary and thus complete through diplomatic channels the work of the Second Hague Conference by giving full effect to its first recommendation."

It is understood that the replies to this note indicated a willingness to the erection of the court as a separate institution, not as a part of the Prize Court, but by employing for this purpose the method of composition of this latter tribunal. This would mean that each signatory of the Prize Court Convention, or that each power willing to form the court, should appoint a judge and a deputy; that the judges of the larger powers should sit during the life of the convention, whereas the judges of the other powers would sit by a system of rotation for shorter periods. But even although this method were acceptable to the large powers, there is apparently an objection to it on the part of the smaller states, and there is a difficulty in the way, even if the objection should be overcome, because this method of composition presupposes the definitive establishment of the Prize Court, which cannot take place, it would seem, until Great Britain ratifies the Prize Court Convention and the Declaration of London, upon which the creation of the court depends. It is, of course, theoretically possible that the Court of Arbitral Justice might be constituted by adopting the method of the Prize Court, but it is believed that the powers would be unwilling to establish the Arbitral Court until the Prize Court itself were in being.

Objections Raised to Proposed Court. So much for the difficulty; next as to the objection. A method similar to that of appointing the judges of the Prize Court was proposed at the Conference for the Court of Arbitral Justice and was rejected. It may be thought strange that a method practically identical should succeed in one case and fail in the other. It may be said that the smaller states were willing to yield a point in the matter of the Prize Court, because they were not interested in it to the same extent as in the Court of Arbitral Justice, although it is believed that in case of war the judgments of the Prize Court would affect neutral rights and duties throughout the world, and that all states would necessarily be interested in it, as they would be affected by its decisions. It may be said again that there was a difference between the two courts, as the jurisdiction of the Prize Court is necessarily limited to prize cases, whereas the Court of Arbitral Justice, without jurisdiction, is nevertheless of unlimited jurisdiction, because by Article 17 of the draft convention it is declared "competent to deal with all cases submitted to it, in virtue either of the general undertaking to have recourse to arbitration or of a special agreement." For the reason stated this difference seems more specious than real, and yet it is not without foundation, because the proposed court might pass upon all phases of international law other than prize cases, and the nations as a whole are and must be interested in the growth of international law considered as a system of jurisprudence.

However this may be, the fact is that the smaller powers put up with inequality in one case and refused to put up with it in the other. Facts are stubborn things and they cannot be argued away. It may be, however, that if the smaller states were assured that the larger ones would consent to establish the Court of Arbitral Justice by the method of the Prize Court and if they now recognize the importance of the court and the services it would render to them better than they did when the proposal was first made at the Conference, they would consent, or a goodly portion of them might consent, to its establishment, even although they disliked the method. This is a matter, however, of conjecture, upon which no opinion can be expressed in the absence of definite information. It should be said, however, in this connection that the partisans of the Court of Arbitral Justice did not insist upon the creation of the court by all the powers, as they knew from the views expressed in debate that the consent of all was impossible, and they framed the recommendation for its constitution through diplomatic channels in such a way that it might be instituted by any number of powers willing to co-operate in its establishment, without, however, attempting to fix the number. This is pointed out in more than one passage of the official report of the American delegation, and, in view of the leading rôle of the American delegation, its views are entitled to more than ordinary weight. Thus, " it follows, therefore, that the powers wishing to establish the court are free to adopt the project of convention, agree upon the method of choosing the judges, and establish the court at The Hague for the trial of cases submitted by the contracting powers." And in a later passage it is said that—

" From this brief exposition it is evident that the foundations of a Permanent Court have been broadly and firmly laid; that the organization, jurisdiction and procedure have been drafted and recommended in the form of a code which the powers or any number of them may accept and, by agreeing upon the appointment of judges, call into being a court at once permanent and international. A little time, a little patience, and the great work is accomplished."

It is not the purpose of this article to restate either the various means which have been suggested to establish the court, as Mr. Choate's address on this subject is printed in the appendix, or to propose methods other than those heretofore suggested.

It seems advisable, however, to call attention to two methods of constituting the court: First, by the method of election, should the nations care to adopt this method, as urged by Mr. Choate; and second, the method of selection upon recommendation of the governments, a method advocated by Dutch publicists since the adjournment of the Conference. Supposing that the court was to consist of fifteen judges, Mr. Choate suggested the following plan in order to meet the desire of the smaller nations that each nation should participate upon an absolute equality in the choice of the judges. Thus:

" ARTICLE 1. Every signatory power shall have the privilege of appointing a judge and an assistant qualified for and disposed to accept such positions and to transmit the names to the international bureau.

" ARTICLE 2. The bureau, that being the case, shall make a

list of all the proposed judges and assistants, with indication of the nations proposing them, and shall transmit it to all the signatory powers.

"ARTICLE 3. Each signatory power shall signify to the bureau which one of the judges and assistants thus named it chooses, each nation voting for fifteen judges and fifteen assistants at the same time.

"ARTICLE 4. The bureau, on receiving the list thus voted for, shall make out a list of the names of the fifteen judges and of the fifteen assistants having received the greatest number of votes."

The second method is similar to but not identical with this, and possesses the advantage of having the nations as a whole pass upon the judges who have been recommended by the nations acting as individual units. Thus, each nation recommends to the Administrative Council of the Permanent Court of Arbitration of The Hague, composed of the diplomatic agents accredited to Holland, one or more persons possessing the qualifications of judges. The Administrative Council then selects from the persons thus recommended the number of judges necessary to constitute the court. Either method would, it is believed, result in the formation of a court worthy of the confidence of the nations, but the latter has the advantage of selection, which the first does not possess, and of election, which is common to both. The difficulty in each case, however, is the same, in that the nation does not directly appoint the judge.

Proposal of Court for Limited Number of Powers.
It is not, however, essential that the court should be formed in the first instance for the nations as a whole, and it is deemed proper in this connection to show how it could be established for a limited number of powers, willing to institute it for themselves, without seeking directly or indirectly to persuade the powers unwilling to constitute it to become parties to it—in other words, to try the experiment upon a smaller scale, for we must admit that an international court is an experiment, before attempting it upon a large scale, in the hope that experience will demonstrate the usefulness of the court and the appropriate method of constituting it for all members of the society of nations that take an interest in the

development of international law and its application to concrete cases involving such law. Such a tribunal would be temporary in the sense that it might be replaced by the larger court, should an agreement be reached upon its constitution, and the writer ventures the suggestion that the attempt should be made in the very near future, so that before the meeting of the Third Conference it should be found in existence, because, in the first place, it is easier to modify an existing institution than to create one out of whole cloth, if the expression be allowed, and because, in the second place, the creation and successful operation of such a court would insure the inclusion of the project in the program of the Third Conference, would concentrate attention upon it, and force the governments to consider it in advance of the meeting of the Conference, which would in all probability secure its definitive establishment by the delegates to the Third Conference.

It has been said that the larger powers are, it is believed, willing to constitute the court, if they are assured of permanent representation in it, as in the case of the Prize Court. If these larger powers —eight in number, namely, Germany, United States, Austria-Hungary, France, Great Britain, Italy, Japan and Russia—would agree to constitute the court for themselves, the question of equality of representation would not arise, as each would naturally appoint a judge in a court created by them. In this case the same result would be accomplished, as far as the larger powers were concerned, as if the Prize Court had been established with the jurisdiction and functions of the Court of Arbitral Justice, or as if the Arbitral Court had been instituted according to the method adopted by the Prize Court Convention for the composition of that court. It would not be national, although national members would be appointed; it would be international, in the sense that it would deal with international problems, although it would only be the court of the nations composing it. It could, therefore, be called with perfect propriety an international court, although it would not be the court of all the nations. There could be no doubt that such a tribunal would be a good thing in itself and the services it would render would undoubtedly make it easier to create a court of the society of nations, because created by the society, and a great impetus would be given to the formation of this larger court, if it were provided that a non-contracting nation might submit its disputes with a contracting nation to the court, or if the two non-contracting nations could avail themselves of it. In such a case each non-contracting nation might appoint a judge for the trial of the case in which it was interested. This could be done without violating the principle of equality, because, even if the dispute were between a contracting and a non-contracting nation, the submission to the court would mean the submission of the nations in litigation to the judgment of the judges whom they had not chosen, but in which for the trial of the particular case they were equally represented.

The advantages of such a provision are, it is believed, clear without argument. It would convince the world at large that the eight nations were genuinely interested in the administration of international justice, not only so far as they themselves were concerned, but by non-contracting nations as well. It would eliminate the criticism of exclusiveness, which otherwise might be made. It would show their confidence in judicial procedure by adopting it for themselves, and their generosity in offering its services to the nations generally would show their interest in the advancement of the great cause of judicial settlement. It would have the inestimable advantage of trying the experiment under the most favorable conditions, because it is not open to question that the eight great nations possess jurists worthy of the great office of international judges, and it cannot be doubted that the gravity of the experiment and the importance of the interests involved would compel the appointment of competent judges, for the contracting nations would not consider for a moment the reference of their mutual disputes to an incompetent or inferior tribunal. This proposition is based upon the fact that the larger powers are convinced of the utility of such a court, and the fact that the original proposers are still interested in its institution leads to the conclusion that the other large powers with which their relations are close, intimate and confidential would, without urging or persuasion, co-operate with them in the establishment of the court.

It is believed that the institution and successful operation of the court would not merely justify the powers in establishing it, but would convince non-contracting powers of its utility, which

perhaps hesitate to pledge themselves to judicial settlement. Theory is one thing; practice is another, and practical demonstration is, with nations as with individuals, more conclusive than theoretical exposition. A few cases decided by the court according to judicial standards would convince the doubting, just as the scruples of St. Thomas were removed.

So far a court of eight has been suggested, but it is self-evident that a ninth should be invited to participate. It would indeed be a sorry feast if the host were overlooked. As the seat of the proposed court—and indeed as the centre of internationalism—Holland has claims which cannot be gainsaid, and in all that goes to make up civilization it certainly stands on an equality with the eight greater powers.

A proposal to give effect to this suggestion is printed in the appendix.

If it could properly be said in 1907 at the meeting of the Second Conference that the time was not ripe for the formation of an international court of justice of a permanent nature, composed of judges chosen in advance of the litigation, this objection, however weighty then, has lost its force in 1914. Publicists of the greatest standing and influence have confessed their faith in favor of it, learned bodies and popular assemblies have advocated it, and the American Society for Judicial Settlement of International Disputes has been formed in the United States, which numbers among its members the élite of the land. In a recent and very valuable work entitled " The Problem of an International Court of Justice " the well-known German publicist, Dr. Hans Wehberg, has stated at length the advantages and difficulties attending the institution of such a tribunal, and has shown the preponderance of professional opinion in its favor. The Institute of International Law, composed of the leading publicists of the world, at its Christiania session in 1912 unanimously declared for it, and adopted the following resolution:

" While recognizing the great value of the Court of Arbitration, instituted by the Peace Conference in 1899, to international justice and the maintenance of peace, the Institute of International Law—

" In order to facilitate and to hasten recourse to arbitration;

to assure the settlement of differences of a legal nature by arbiters representing the different systems of legislation and of jurisprudence;

"In order to reinforce the authority of the tribunals in the eyes of the representatives of the parties in controversy by having the members of the tribunal known to them in advance, and likewise to increase the moral force of the decision by having it rendered by a larger number and by the authority of arbiters recognized by the totality of the States;

"In order to resolve, in case of a treaty of compulsory arbitration containing a clause to this effect, the doubts which might arise as to whether or not a particular controversy belongs to the category of questions subject to compulsory arbitration under the treaty;

"In order to create a Court of Appeals for decisions rendered by tribunals constituted otherwise than in conformity with the rules of the Hague Convention, in case the special *compromis* should provide for the possibility of such a revision;

"Considers it highly desirable that satisfaction be given to the first *voeu* adopted by the Second Peace Conference in favor of the establishment of a Court of Arbitral Justice."

The Mohonk Conference on International Arbitration may be taken as the type of a popular assembly, although it is composed of chosen spirits. Year after year it has adopted resolutions favoring the establishment of the court, and at its last session (May, 1914) it affirmed its previous action by the following resolution:

"We recommend that in addition to the present Permanent Court of Arbitration at The Hague, as established under the conventions of 1899 and 1907, there be established as soon as practicable, among such powers as may agree thereto, a court with a determinate personnel, as advised by the Second Hague Conference."

The movement in favor of judicial settlement is more fortunate than most reforms, for their defense is ordinarily entrusted to weak hands and their partisans are frequently regarded as dreamers of dreams and as men without experience in the actual conduct of affairs. In the present instance the proposal for the establishment of an international court of justice was made by no less a person than Elihu Root, when Secretary of State, and as a Senator of the

United States he still champions the cause which he created. We may, if we please, shrug our shoulders at resolutions of scientific societies such as the Institute of International Law, or of popular assemblies such as the Mohonk Conference, but a man must be very sure of himself who would endeavor to dispute the following weighty words spoken by Mr. Root at the opening meeting of the American Society for Judicial Settlement of International Disputes in 1910:

"But there are some difficulties about arbitration—practical difficulties in the way of settling questions. I have said many times and in many places that I do not think the difficulty that stands in the way of arbitration to-day is an unwillingness on the part of the civilized nations of the earth to submit their disputes to impartial decision. I think the difficulty is a doubt on the part of civilized nations as to getting an impartial decision. And that doubt arises from some characteristics of arbitral tribunals, which are very difficult to avoid.

"In the first place, these tribunals are ordinarily made up by selecting publicists, men of public affairs, great civil servants, members of the foreign offices, men trained to diplomacy; and the inevitable tendency is, and the result often has been, in the majority of cases, that the arbitral tribunal simply substitutes itself for the negotiators of the two parties, and negotiates a settlement. Well, that is quite a different thing from submitting your views of right and wrong, your views of the facts and the law on which you base your claims to right, to the decision of a tribunal, of a court. It is merely handing over your interests to somebody to negotiate for you; and there is a very widespread reluctance to do that in regard to many cases; and the nearer the question at issue approaches the verge of the field of policy, the stronger the objection to doing that.

"Another difficulty is that the arbitral tribunals, of course being made up largely of members from other countries, the real decision ordinarily being made by arbiters who come from other countries, and not from the countries concerned, questions have to be presented to men trained under different systems of law, with different ways of thinking and of looking at matters. There is a very wide difference between the way in which a civil lawyer and a common-law lawyer will approach a subject, and it is sometimes pretty hard for them to understand each other, even though they speak the same language, while if they speak different languages it is still more difficult.

" Another difficulty is that a large part of the rules of international law are still vague and undetermined, and upon many of them, and especially upon those out of which controversy is most likely to arise, different countries take different views as to what the law is and ought to be. And no one can tell how one of these extemporized tribunals, picked at haphazard, or upon the best information the negotiators of two countries can get—no one can tell what views they are going to take about questions of international law, or how they are going to approach subjects and deal with them.

" Now it has seemed to me very clear that in view of these practical difficulties standing in the way of our present system of arbitration, the next step by which the system of peaceable settlement of international disputes can be advanced, the pathway along which it can be pressed forward to universal acceptance and use, is to substitute for the kind of arbitration we have now, in which the arbitrators proceed according to their ideas of diplomatic obligation, real courts where judges, acting under the sanctity of the judicial oath, pass upon the rights of countries, as judges pass upon the rights of individuals, in accordance with the facts as found and the law as established. With such tribunals, which are continuous, and composed of judges who make it their life business, you will soon develop a bench composed of men who have become familiar with the ways in which the people of every country do their business and do their thinking, and you will have a gradual growth of definite rules, of fixed interpretation, and of established precedents, according to which you may know your case will be decided.

" It is with that view that I have felt grateful to the gentlemen who have been giving their time and efforts to the organization and establishment of this Society. I am sure that it is a step along the scientific and practical method of putting into operation all the principles that we have been preaching and listening to for so many years. It is practical, and I believe it will be effective."

APPENDIX A

(1) MR. CHOATE'S ADDRESS ON THE AMERICAN PROJECT FOR A PERMANENT COURT OF ARBITRAL JUSTICE, AUGUST 1, 1907 [1]

Mr. President:

In commending to the favorable consideration of the subcommission the scheme which our delegation has embodied in a proposition relative to the Permanent Court of Arbitration, I cannot better begin what I have to say than to quote a sentence from the letter of President Roosevelt to Mr. Carnegie on the fifth of April last, which was read at the Peace Conference held at New York. He says:

I hope to see adopted a general arbitration treaty among the nations, and I hope to see the Hague Court greatly increased in power and permanency, and the judges in particular made permanent and given adequate salaries so as to make it increasingly probable that in each case that may come before them they will decide between the nations, great or small, exactly as a judge within our own limits decides between the individuals, great or small, who come before him. Doubtless many other matters will be taken up at The Hague, but it seems to me that this of a general arbitration treaty is perhaps the most important.

And our instructions are to secure, if possible, a plan by which the judges shall be so selected from the different countries that the different systems of law and procedure and the principal languages shall be fairly represented, and that the court shall be made of such dignity, consideration, and rank that the best and ablest jurists will accept appointments to it, and that the whole world will have absolute confidence in its judgments.

There can be no doubt, Mr. President, of the supreme importance of the step in advance which we ask the conference to take in developing and building up, out of the Permanent Court of Arbitration created by the conference of 1899, a tribunal which shall conform to these requirements and satisfy a universal demand which presses upon us from all quarters of the world for the establishment of such a tribunal. The general cause of arbitration as a substitute for wars in the settlement of international differences has advanced by leaps and bounds since the close of the First Peace Conference, and nothing

[1] La Deuxième Conférence Internationale de la Paix, Actes et Documents (1st Commission, 1st Subcommission, August 1, 1907), Vol. II, pp. 309-314 (327-330).

more strongly demonstrates the utility of the great work accomplished by that conference than the general resort of the nations to agreements for arbitration among themselves as the sure means of securing justice and peace and avoiding a resort to the terrible test of war.

Our plan, if adopted, will preserve and perpetuate the excellent work of the First Conference and carry it to its logical conclusion. Following the noble initiative of Lord Pauncefote, that great and wise statesman who was the First Delegate of Great Britain, whose persuasive words upon the subject will never be forgotten, the First Conference, after establishing for all time the principles of arbitration, created a tribunal to which all nations, whether signatory powers or not, might voluntarily resort for the determination of all arbitrations upon which they might agree. But one cannot read the debates which ushered in the taking of that great step by the First Conference without realizing that it was undertaken by that body as a new experiment and not without apprehension, but with an earnest hope that it would serve as a basis, at least, of further advanced work in the same direction by a future conference. The project was as simple as the purpose of it was grand, but, as Mr. Asser has well said in his eloquent speech, it created a court in name only by furnishing a list of jurists and other men of skill in international law from whom the parties to each litigation might select judges to determine the case, who should sit at The Hague according to machinery provided for the purpose, and proceed by certain prescribed methods, if no others were agreed upon by the parties.

We have with us, I believe, as members of the present conference, some seventeen members of the former conference who participated in that great work, and about an equal number of the judges whose names were placed upon the list by the various nations in conformity with the power given them by the convention of 1899. And our present effort is by no means to belittle or detract from their work, but to build upon it a still nobler and more commanding structure, and it is their support that we would seek especially to enlist in this new undertaking.

We do not err, Mr. President, in saying that the work of the First Conference in this regard, noble and far-reaching as it was, has not proved entirely complete and adequate to meet the progressive demands of the nations, and to draw to the Hague Tribunal for decision any great part of the arbitrations that have been agreed upon; and that in the eight years of its existence only four cases have been submitted to it, and of the sixty judges, more or less, who were named as members of the court at least two-thirds have not, as yet, been called upon for any service. It is not easy, or perhaps desirable, at this stage of the discussion to analyze all the causes of the failure of a general or frequent resort by the nations to the Hague Tribunal, but a few of them are so obvious that they may be properly suggested. Certainly it was for no lack of adequate and competent and distinguished judges, for the services they have performed in the four cases which they have considered have been of the highest character, and it is out of those very judges that we propose to constitute our new proposed court.

I am inclined to think that one of the causes which have prevented a more frequent resort of nations to the Hague Tribunal, especially in cases of ordinary or minor importance, has been the expensiveness of a case brought there; and it should be one element of reform that the expense of the court itself, including the salaries of the judges, shall be borne at the common expense of all the signatory powers, so as to furnish to the suitors a court at least free of expense to them, as is the case with suitors of all nations in their national courts.

The fact that there was nothing permanent or continuous or connected in the sessions of the court, or in the adjudication of the cases submitted to it, has been an obvious source of weakness and want of prestige in the tribunal. Each trial it had before it has been wholly independent of every other, and its occasional utterances, widely distant in point of time and disconnected in subject-matter, have not gone far towards constituting a consistent body of international law or of valuable contributions to international law, which ought to emanate from an international tribunal representing the power and might of all the nations. In fact, it has thus far been a court only in name—a framework for the selection of referees for each particular case, never consisting of the same judges. It has done great good as far as it has been permitted to work at all, but our effort should be to try to make a tribunal which shall be the medium of vastly greater and constantly increasing benefit to the nations and to mankind at large.

Let us then seek to develop out of it a permanent court, which shall hold regular and continuous sessions, which shall consist of the same judges, which shall pay due heed to its own decisions, which shall speak with the authority of the united voice of the nations, and gradually build up a system of international law, definite and precise, which shall command the approval and regulate the conduct of the nations. By such a step in advance we shall justify the confidence which has been placed in us and shall make the work of this Second Conference worthy of comparison with that of the conference of 1899.

We have not, Mr. President, in the proposition which we have offered, attempted even to sketch the details of the constitution and powers and character of our proposed court. We have not thought it possible that one nation could of itself prescribe or even suggest such details, but that they should be the result of consultation and conference among all the nations represented in a suitable committee to be appointed by the president to consider them.

The plan proposed by us, Mr. President, does not in the least depart from the voluntary character of the court already established. No nation can be compelled or constrained to come before it, but it will be open for all who desire to settle their differences by peaceful methods and to avoid the terrible consequences and chances of war.

In the first article of our project we suggest that such a permanent court of arbitration ought to be constituted; and that is the great question of principle to be first decided. And to that end we submit that it should be composed of not more than seventeen judges, of whom nine should be a quorum—men who have enjoyed the highest moral consideration and a recognized competence in questions of international law; that they shall be designated and elected by the nations, but in a way prescribed by this entire conference, so that all the nations, great and small, shall have a voice in designating the manner of their choice; and that they shall be chosen from so many different countries as fairly to represent all the different systems of existing law and procedure, all the principal languages of the world, all the great human interests, and a widely distributed geographical character; that they shall be named for a certain number of years, to be decided by the conference, and shall hold their offices until their respective successors, to be chosen as the conference shall prescribe, shall have accepted and qualified.

Our second article, Mr. President, provides that our Permanent Court shall sit annually at The Hague upon a specified date, the same date in each year, to be fixed by the conference, and that they shall remain in session as long as the necessity of the business that shall come before them may require; that they shall appoint their own officers and, except as this or the preceding conference prescribes, shall regulate their own procedure; that every decision of the court shall be by a majority of voices, and that nine members shall constitute a quorum, although this number is subject to the decision of the conference.

We desire that the judges shall be of equal rank, shall enjoy diplomatic immunity, and shall receive a salary, to be paid out of the common purse of the nations, sufficient to justify them in devoting to the consideration of the business of the court all the time that shall be necessary.

By the third article we express our preference that in no case, unless the parties otherwise agree, shall any judge of the court take part in the consideration or decision of any matter coming before the court to which his own nation shall be a party. In other words, Mr. President, we would have it in all respects strictly a court of justice, and not partake in the least of the nature of a joint commission.

By the fourth article we would make the jurisdiction of this Permanent Court large enough to embrace the hearing and decision of all cases involving differences of an international character between sovereign states, which they had not been able to settle by diplomatic methods, and which shall be submitted to it by an agreement of the parties; that it shall have not only original jurisdiction, but that room shall be given to it to entertain appeals, if it should be thought advisable, from other tribunals, and to determine the relative rights, duties, or obligations arising out of the sentences or decrees of commissions of inquiry or specially constituted tribunals of arbitration.

Our fifth article provides that the judges of the court shall be competent to act as judges upon commissions of inquiry or special arbitration tribunals, but in that case, of course, not to sit in review of their own decisions, and that the court shall have power to entertain and dispose of any international controversy that shall be submitted to it by the powers.

And finally, by Article 6, that its membership shall be made up as far as possible out of the membership of the existing court, from those judges who have been or shall be named by the parties now constituting the present conference, in conformity with the rules which this conference shall finally prescribe.

Mr. President, with all the earnestness of which we are capable, and with a solemn sense of the obligations and responsibilities resting upon us as members of this conference, which in a certain sense holds in its hand the fate and fortunes of the nations, we commend the scheme which we have thus proposed to the careful consideration of our sister nations. We cherish no pride of opinion as to any point or feature that we have suggested in regard to the constitution and powers of the court. We are ready to yield any or all of them for the sake of harmony, but we do insist that this great gathering of the representatives of all the nations will be false to its trust, and will deserve that the seal of condemnation shall be set upon its work, if it does not strain every nerve to bring about the establishment of some such great and permanent tribunal which shall, by its supreme authority, compel the attention and deference of the nations that we represent, and bring to final adjudication before it differences of an international character that shall arise between them, and whose decisions shall be appealed to as time progresses for the determination of all questions of international law.

Let us, then, Mr. President, make a supreme effort to attain not harmony only, but complete unanimity in the accomplishment of this great measure, which will contribute more than anything else we can do to establish justice and peace on everlasting foundations.

The commission will distinctly understand that our proposed court, if established, will not destroy but will only supplement the existing court, established by the conference of 1899, and that any nations who desire it may still resort to the method of selecting arbitrators there provided.

Gentlemen, it is now six weeks since we first assembled. There is certainly no time to lose. We have done much to regulate war, but very little to prevent it. Let us unite on this great pacific measure and satisfy the world that this Second Conference really intends that hereafter peace and not war shall be the normal condition of civilized nations.

(2) MR. SCOTT'S ADDRESS ON THE ELEMENTS ENTERING INTO THE COMPOSITION OF AN INTERNATIONAL COURT OF ARBITRAL JUSTICE, AUGUST 1, 1907.[1]

In opening the National Arbitration and Peace Congress in the city of New York, on the fifteenth day of April, 1907, the Hon. Elihu Root, Secretary of State for the United States of America, expressed, in a few apt paragraphs, the causes which have worked against general arbitration and the reasons which have prevented a more frequent recourse to the Permanent Tribunal of Arbitration at The Hague. I therefore beg to quote the following passages from his address:

It has seemed to me that the great obstacle to the universal adoption of arbitration is not the unwillingness of civilized nations to submit their disputes to the decision of an impartial tribunal; it is rather an apprehension that the tribunal selected will not be impartial. In a dispatch to Sir Julian Pauncefote, dated March 5, 1896, Lord Salisbury stated the difficulty. He said that
" If the matter in controversy is important, so that defeat is a serious blow to the credit or the power of the litigant who is worsted, that interest becomes a more or less keen partisanship. According to their sympathies, men wish for the victory of one side or another. Such conflicting sympathies interfered most formidably with the choice of an impartial arbitrator. It would be too invidious to specify the various forms of bias by which, in any important controversy between two great powers, the other members of the commonwealth of nations are visibly affected. In the existing condition of international sentiment each great power could point to nations whose admission to any jury, by whom its interests were to be tried, it would be bound to challenge; and in a litigation between two great powers the rival challenges would pretty well exhaust the catalogue of the nations from which competent and suitable arbiters could be drawn. It would be easy, but scarcely decorous, to illustrate the statement by examples. They will occur to any one's mind who attempts to construct a panel of nations capable of providing competent arbitrators, and will consider how many of them would command equal confidence from any two litigating powers.
" This is the difficulty which stands in the way of unrestricted arbitration. By whatever plan the tribunal is selected, the end of it must be that issues in which the litigant states are most deeply interested will be decided by the will of one man, and that man a foreigner. He has no jury to find his facts; he has no court of appeals to correct his law; and he is sure to be credited, justly or not, with a leaning to one litigant or the other."
The feeling which Lord Salisbury so well expressed is, I think, the great stumbling-block in the way of arbitration. The essential fact which supports that feeling is that arbitration too often acts diplomatically rather than judicially; they consider themselves as belonging to diplomacy rather than to jurisprudence; they measure their responsibility and their duty by the traditions, the sentiments, and the sense of honorable obligation which has grown up in centuries of diplomatic intercourse, rather than by the traditions, the sentiments, and the sense of honorable obligation which characterizes the judicial department of civilized nations. Instead of the sense of responsibility for impartial judgment, which weighs upon the judicial officers of every civilized country, and which is enforced by the honor and self-respect of every upright judge, an international arbitration is often regarded as an occasion for diplomatic adjustment. Granting that the diplomats who are engaged in an arbitration have the purest motives; that they act in accordance with the policy they deem to be best

[1] La Deuxième Conférence Internationale de la Paix, Actes et Documents (1st Commission, 1st Subcommission, August 1, 1907), Vol. II, pp. 313-321.

for the nations concerned in the controversy; assuming that they thrust aside entirely in their consideration any interests which their own countries may have in the controversy or in securing the favor or averting the displeasure of the parties before them, nevertheless it remains that in such an arbitration the litigant nations find that questions of policy, and not simple questions of fact and law, are submitted to alien determination, and an appreciable part of that sovereignty which it is the function of every nation to exercise for itself in determining its own policy is transferred to the arbitrators. . . .

What we need for the further development of arbitration is the substitution of judicial action for diplomatic action, the substitution of judicial sense of responsibility for diplomatic sense of responsibility. We need for arbitrators not distinguished public men concerned in all the international questions of the day, but judges who will be interested only in the question appearing upon the record before them. Plainly this end is to be attained by the establishment of a court of permanent judges, who will have no other occupation and no other interest but the exercise of the judicial faculty under the sanction of that high sense of responsibility which has made the courts of justice in the civilized nations of the world the exponents of all that is best and noblest in modern civilization.

It is a familiar doctrine that the shoemaker should stick to his last and that he should not go beyond it. It should be an equally familiar doctrine that lawyers and jurists of reputation are preëminently qualified to deal with questions relating to the organization and development of a court of justice. The opinion is not expressed, either directly or indirectly, that the layman should not have views upon this subject, and express them, but it would seem to be unarguable that the advice of the bench and the bar should be determinative in all questions relating to courts of justice.

The plan which the American delegation has had the honor to lay before the conference is the result of direct instructions from the Secretary of State, who is not only a lawyer of distinction but a leader of the bar. The explanation of the general principles relating to the establishment of a permanent court comes from our distinguished First Delegate, who led the American bar as long as he chose to remain in active practice.

It would seem, therefore, that a project outlined by one practitioner of distinction, and commended to your careful consideration by another no less distinguished member of the profession, must possess qualities which commend it to the consideration of the profession at large.

The American people, rightly or wrongly, are regarded as preëminently practical, and a project which commands their unanimous support, because it expresses their innermost desire, must be practical in the broadest sense of the term. But we believe that the project for the establishment of a permanent court will not merely commend itself to practitioners, but that it is susceptible of theoretical defense.

Before entering upon the detailed exposition of the project and presenting the fundamental principles underlying the proposed permanent court, I desire to call attention to the present court and to show its strength and its weakness, in order that it may appear that our project develops the strength on the one hand and eliminates the weakness on the other.

The strength of the work of 1899 lies in the *idea* of a court for the settlement of international differences; its weakness consists in the fact that the machinery provided is inadequate for its realization.

I quote the following articles from the convention of 1899:

ARTICLE 15. International arbitration has for its object the settlement of differences between states by judges of their own choice, and on the basis of respect for law.

ARTICLE 16. In questions of a legal nature, especially in the interpretation or application of international conventions, arbitration is recognized by the signatory powers as the most effective, and at the same time the most equitable, means of settling disputes which diplomacy has failed to settle.

ARTICLE 20. With the object of facilitating immediate recourse to arbitration for international differences which it has not been possible to settle by diplomacy, the signatory powers undertake to organize a permanent court of arbitration, accessible at all times, and operating, unless otherwise stipulated by the parties, in accordance with the rules of procedure inserted in the present convention.

The intent of the framers of this remarkable convention is evident: Arbitration is to take up the task of settlement where diplomacy has failed, and reason thus thrusts itself between negotiation and the sword.

The signatory powers agreed to organize a permanent court of arbitration, and this court, so organized, was to be accessible at all times. It is common knowledge that no permanent court exists because no permanent court ever was established under the convention, and it necessarily follows that if a permanent court does not exist, it is not accessible at all times, or indeed at any time. The most that can be said is that the signatory powers furnished a list of judges from which, as occasion required, a temporary tribunal of arbitration might be composed.

It would further appear that the judges so appointed by the signatory powers were not necessarily judges in the legal sense of the word, but might be jurists, negotiators, diplomatists, or politicians specially detailed. In a word, the Permanent Court is not permanent because it is not composed of permanent judges; it is not accessible because it has to be constituted for each case; it is not a court because it is not composed of judges.

A careful examination of the sections previously quoted shows beyond peradventure that the framers contemplated the establishment of a court of justice to which differences of an international nature might be submitted for judicial consideration and decision.

Article 15 speaks of "judges of their choice," and indicates in no uncertain measure that the decision is to be based upon "respect of law." Article 16 lays stress upon questions of a judicial nature and declares that arbitration is recognized as the most efficacious and the most equitable method of settling conflicts of this nature.

It requires neither argument nor intellectual acumen to discover the intent of the convention in the wording and in the spirit of the act itself.

To decide as a judge, and according to law, it is evident that a court should be constituted, and it is also evident that the court should sit as a judicial, not as a diplomatic or political, tribunal. Questions of special national interest should be excluded because the intent clearly is to decide a controversy not by national law but by international law. A court is not a branch of the foreign office, nor is it a chancellery. Questions of a political nature should likewise be excluded, for a court is neither a deliberative nor a legislative assembly. It neither makes laws nor determines a policy. Its supreme function is to interpret and to apply the law to a concrete case.

The court, therefore, is a judicial body composed of judges whose duty it is to examine the case presented, to weigh evidence, and thus establish the facts involved, and to the facts thus found to apply a principle of law, thus forming the judgment. It follows, then, that only questions capable of judicial treatment should be submitted, and that the duty of the judge should be limited to the formation of judgments. The desideratum is that a law and its interpretation should be certain, and certainty of judgment is possible only when strictly judicial questions are presented to the court. Upon a given state of facts you may predicate a judgment. If special interests be introduced, if political questions be involved, the judgment of a court must be as involved and confused as the special interests and political questions.

In stating boldly that the court should not deal with questions of special national interest, nor with questions of national policy, and in expressing the opinion that judges should decide according to the law as judges, not as negotiators or diplomats, it is not meant to suggest that experience in political or diplomatic life would disqualify a judge for the performance of judicial duties. As the politician deals with political questions, he is clearly out of place in a court of justice, although a broad experience in political affairs may strengthen the judgment of the individual judge and thus enhance his efficiency. The diplomat, as such, is likewise out of place in a court of justice, because we do not wish to weigh the claim of one against the other and strike a balance. A compromise is out of place, and negotiations are excluded. Experience, however, in diplomatic life is of value, indeed of great value, but it can only enlarge the view and thus increase the usefulness of the judge individually. Political experience and diplomatic training cannot make up for the lack of the judicial mind and the legal way of thought.

It is difficult to conceive of a court of justice without judges trained in the administration of justice. It is difficult—indeed it is well-nigh impossible—to think of a court without at one and the same time having in mind the jurisdiction of the court. An international court does not compete with a national court. The questions submitted to it are not of a national or municipal character. They are of an international character, to be determined according to international equity and international law. It necessarily follows that the jurisdiction of such a court would be different from the jurisdiction of a national court. The one point in common is that each should have a certain sphere of jurisdiction if it is to function as a court. In what, then, may the jurisdiction of an international court consist? Clearly it can have no original jurisdiction. Its jurisdiction must be conferred upon it specifically, for when created it is as powerless and helpless as the newborn babe. The jurisdiction must be conferred upon it expressly, and it would seem that this may happen in several ways. First, the signatory powers may conclude a *general* treaty of arbitration and may agree that all differences of an international nature shall be considered. Or, second, if the signatory powers do not conclude a general agreement, the positive jurisdiction of the court may be based upon the several treaties of arbitration already concluded between the nations.

In either case the court will be clothed with a certain jurisdiction; for, as the powers have agreed collectively or singly to refer certain matters to the Permanent Court, it follows that the court possesses the competence to examine these. In a word, the court possesses obligatory jurisdiction in certain defined and ascertained cases.

But it may well happen that nations may, in the absence of a treaty of arbitration, be willing to submit special differences arising between them to the judgment and determination of the court. As the jurisdiction in such cases would be occasional, and as it would depend wholly upon the volition of the parties in controversy, it may be called voluntary or facultative jurisdiction. It is a matter of no great importance whether the jurisdiction is obligatory or whether it is facultative, provided only that questions be submitted to the court for their determination. And it is believed that particular questions will be submitted to the court as soon as the court justifies its existence, and that these submissions will be more frequent in proportion as the court wins universal confidence and trust. It is, therefore, no objection to the court that the obligatory jurisdiction may be small, provided only that the facultative jurisdiction be large. And it will, in the nature of things, be large if the court be permanent, if it be composed of judges, and if the decisions of the judges satisfy the judicial conscience.

The very permanency of the court will go far to create the confidence which a line of carefully considered and authoritative precedents will justify. For it is important that the court and its personnel be permanent in order that a permanent body of international doctrine be developed. Each decision will be a milestone in the line of progress and will forecast a highly developed, comprehensive, and universal system of international law. But to create a precedent and to secure its recognition it is necessary that the decision itself shall be impartial, according to the law of the case, and the surroundings of the court should be such as to allay suspicion of partiality. Judges of training and experience, serving for years instead of for a few weeks, will develop a judicial faculty, even although its presence be not so marked at the date of appointment. An arbiter, chosen for a particular purpose by a particular government, after weighing his strength and his weakness, after an examination of his writings or utterances, may be discredited in advance and doubts cast upon his impartiality, because it is well known that nations as well as men are inclined to appoint those favorable, not those unfavorable, to their views. There is, therefore, great danger that the arbiter be but slightly removed from the advocate; whereas the judge, by virtue of his tenure, cannot, in the nature of things, be exposed to this danger or to this criticism. It is not too much to say, therefore, that the confidence which the court may inspire will depend as much upon the permanence of tenure as upon the character and attainments of the individual judges.

It is probable that the views already presented may meet with general acceptance, but the important question still remains, How is this Permanent Court, composed of judges, to be constituted? No attempt is made to disguise the difficulty and importance of this question; for if it were an easy task, we would not be engaged in discussing it in this year of grace 1907.

It is obvious at the outstart that a court, to be truly international, should represent not only one or many but all nations. It is equally obvious that a court composed of a single representative from each independent and sovereign nation would be unwieldy. Forty-five judges, sitting together, might compose a judicial assembly; they would not constitute a court. And our purpose is to establish a court, not to call into existence a judicial assembly.

In international law all states are equal. As our great Chief Justice Marshall said:

No principle of general law is more universally acknowledged than the perfect equality of nations. Russia and Geneva have equal rights. It results from this equality that no one can rightfully impose a rule on another. Each legislates itself, and its legislation can operate on itself alone (The *Antelope*, 1825, 10 Wheaton, 66, *122*).

It follows, then, that however desirable a permanent court may be, it cannot be imposed upon any nation. The court can only exist for this nation by reason of its express consent. If it be said that all states are equal, it necessarily follows that the conception of great and small powers finds no place in a correct system of international law. It is only when we leave the realm of law and face brute force that inequality appears. It is only when the sword is thrown upon the scales of justice that the balance tips; or, to quote the fine words of our honored president, M. Léon Bourgeois, uttered in a moment of inspiration:

Gentlemen, what is now the rule among individual men will hereafter obtain among nations. Such international institutions as these will be the protection of the weak against the powerful. In the conflicts of brute force, where fighters of flesh and with steel are in line, we may speak of great powers and small, of weak and of mighty. When swords are thrown in the balance, one side may easily outweigh the other. But in the weighing of rights and ideas disparity ceases, and the rights of the smallest and the weakest powers count as much in the scales as those of the mightiest.

In matters of justice there can be no distinction, for every state, be it large or small, has an equal interest that justice be done. If, therefore, a permanent court be constructed upon the basis of abstract right, equality, and justice, it would follow that each state would sit, of right, within an international tribunal, and we will be confronted with a list of judges—with a panel, not a court. Recognizing the equality of right and the equality of interest in law, and giving full effect to this equality in the constitution of a permanent court, we must yet find some other principle upon which to base it if we wish to erect a small court of a permanent nature.

Fortunately another principle exists. While all states are equal in international law, and while their interest in justice is the same, or should be the same, there is a great difference between nations considered from the standpoint of material interests. And fortunately material interests are independent of the question of power, for power, in the international sense of the word, means physical force, and physical force is alien to the conception of right. The principle of construction cannot be based upon the relative strength or weakness of nations; but while nations have an equal interest in justice in the abstract, this interest may manifest itself more frequently in the concrete. The interests of a large and populous state are widespread, indeed universal, and complications and differences are most likely to arise where these interests come into conflict. It cannot be said that lawsuits bear a mathematical and constant relation to population. A state of thirty millions may not have six times as many lawsuits as a state of five millions, and it is to be hoped that this is not so. But there is a sensible relation between population, wealth, and industry on the one hand and lawsuits on the other. If we compare the states of the American Union, we will see at a glance that the law reports of the state of New York compared with the law reports of Rhode Island and Delaware, our smallest states in population as well as in size, show the greater material interest in the state of New York in courts of justice. Population and the business necessarily arising and inseparable from population make a recourse to the courts of justice in New York the rule, while in the smaller states it would seem to be the exception. It follows, therefore, in practice as in theory, that the state of New York has many more law courts and infinitely more judges, simply because the needs of the population are in this way met.

The foregoing illustration would apply to an international as well as to a municipal or national court. The greater the population, the greater the business; the greater the business, the more frequent the conflict of interests involving a recourse to a court of justice. An international court would seem to be at the present day as much a necessity as the municipal court is a necessity, for international interests, in their infinite variety and complexity, would or should be referred to an international court, just as conflicts arising wholly within one jurisdiction are referred to the municipal court of the particular nation in question. The municipal court is created to meet the national need. An international court should be created and exist to meet the international need, and it is not to be expected that nations with great material interests will be content to support or accept an international court which does not recognize these interests, and in which these interests are not represented. Material interests may, however, be very large or may be very small, and the difficulty of estimating the value of a particular interest, and the extent to which it should find representation in a court, would seem to render it either impossible or inexpedient as a basis for the constitution of an international court.

It has been stated—and any geographer or gazetteer will furnish the proof— that material interests and populations go hand in hand; that a large population has, by reason of its largeness, material needs which must be satisfied; that industry and commerce spring up to meet these needs, and in satisfying them wealth results. If, therefore, population draws to itself industry and commerce, and if courts of justice, in a civil and commercial sense, are created to resolve commercial or civic differences, it would seem that population (which is easily determinable) may be chosen as a basis of representation because of the direct relation existing between population on the one hand and industry and commerce on the other. Population is a natural principle, and a court of justice based upon the principle of population thus recognizes an actual and natural principle. Business interests are at one and the same time likewise recognized, and justice is administered clearly and impartially, if only the personnel of the court be properly selected.

Admitting that population may be taken as an element upon which to constitute an international court, it is necessary to state, with clearness and precision, the population which shall give a unit of representation. If the required population be very small, it follows that the membership of the court, chosen in accordance with population, will be very large; and, on the other hand, if a very high degree of population be required, it follows that the membership of the court will be correspondingly small. But whatever unit be chosen, no state, however populous, should have more than one member in the court, for a single member calls attention to the existence of the state as a political unit, and represents at one and the same time its population, industry, and commerce.

It is, therefore, necessary to choose the golden mean in such a way that the membership of the court shall not be so large as to make it unwieldy, nor so small as to leave unrepresented important international interests. It seems probable that a court composed of fifteen or sixteen judges would be manageable, and adequate for all our present international needs.

If it be true that population and material interests bear a sensible proportion to each other, it follows that the entire population of a country should be included, and that its right to representation should depend upon this combined population, for it is not merely the interests of the home country, but the interests of the colonies, that come before courts of justice.

If it be admitted that population is a satisfactory basis upon which to erect a substantial and permanent court of arbitration, it would not follow that we had composed the court, although we had taken a step toward it by establishing approximately the number of judges of the court. We must determine the law to be enforced. The problem here is complicated by the fact that many systems of law exist and that these various systems must find adequate representation. As a rule, a single system of law obtains in a municipal court; another system obtains in another court. These two systems, administered in one and the same court, would not make the tribunal a court of international law; for, to be truly international, it must embrace the various systems of the world. When this is done it becomes a world court. If the Permanent Court of Arbitration is to judge according to equity and international law, it must not be the equity of any one system, but the equity which is the resultant of the various systems of law. Just as the individual rarely frees himself from his environment, so the jurist is influenced by his system of law and the training in it. Supposing, therefore, that each is influenced by his training; it is necessary to have judges trained in the various systems of law in order that the equity administered by the court may be truly the spirit of the laws. For the purpose of the Permanent Court of Arbitration municipal law must be internationalized. In this case, and in this case only, can the judgment be equitable in any international sense, and the judgment so formed will be based upon international equity as well as international law.

It is stated that a jurist is the product of his training. It is likewise true that the individual is influenced by the environment, and possesses, in a higher or less degree, the characteristics of his nation. It would be futile—if, indeed, it were possible—to denationalize a judge. But the presence in the court of judges trained in the various systems of law, and representing in their intellectual development characteristics of their respective nations, would go far towards engendering an international spirit.

The project which the American delegation has the honor to present recognizes the existence of the various systems of law and gives adequate representation to them.

For example, the Roman law, constituting the basis of so many European systems, would be represented in its present and modified forms. The common law of England would be represented, and the common law of England as modified in the western world would not be overlooked. The nations of Europe which have given law to the western world would sit, of right, in the court, and at one and the same time the modifications of this law, to meet the needs of the New World, would be before the court. For example, the law of Spain—the source of law in Latin America—would appear both in its European and American form.

The question of language is one of great difficulty, and language as such should be represented in the court. To one sitting in the conference day by day and observing the difficulty with which the idea clothes itself in French form, it must be a matter of great importance that the languages should find representation in the court, so that the judge and client may be upon speaking terms.

If a question of Spanish law is involved, it is important that the judge understand Spanish. If a matter of Russian law be under consideration, a knowledge of Russian might well be fundamental. An examination of the American project shows that the principle of population does ample justice to the languages most widely spoken at the present day.

Finally, a court, to be international, must take note of the existence of the nations of the world, and these nations must find adequate representation in the court. The principle of population adopted shows that the four quarters of the globe would be represented in the court.

It may have seemed strange, at first sight, that the American project bases itself upon the principle of population, but when it is seen that the principle of population does justice to the industry and commerce of the world; that it likewise represents the various systems of law; that it includes within itself the languages, and that political geography is not overlooked, it becomes at once evident that the principle of population was selected not for any virtue of its own but because it adequately and equitably represents and embodies the elements essential to the constitution and operation of a permanent court of arbitration.

In a word, our principle recognizes the existence of nations, and their continued existence, as political units, but declares solemnly that for the purposes of justice there is but one people.

In the observations which I have had the honor to submit I have dwelt upon the fundamental underlying principles of the American project without considering matters of detail. Did time permit, it could easily be shown how a permanent court of arbitration, composed of fifteen or sixteen judges, would fulfill the mission now confided to other and variously constituted bodies.

For example, should parties to a controversy desire a summary proceeding, they might request a special detail of three or five judges from the Permanent Court of Arbitration by striking alternately from the list an equal number until the desired number remained. Powers desiring to form a commission of inquiry for a particular purpose could resort to the Permanent Court of Arbitration and constitute a commission in the above-described manner, and add thereto an equal number of nationals from each of the parties. It would require no great powers of imagination to devise a method by which the personnel of the Permanent Court of Arbitration might be modified to meet regulations and requirements of a court of prize; and finally, by special consent of the parties to a controversy, decisions of commissions of arbitration might be referred to the Permanent Court of Arbitration to be reviewed and revised, or to have the relative duties and liabilities under the findings submitted to further examination.

Without considering further details, and without prolonging a discourse already long, I beg to express the conviction that the mere existence of a permanent court of arbitration, composed of a limited number of judges trained in municipal law and experienced in the law of nations, would be a guarantee of peace. As long as men are what they are, and nations are formed of ordinary men, we shall be exposed to war and rumors of war. The generous and high-minded may seek to ameliorate the evils and misfortunes of armed conflict, but it is certainly a nobler task, and a more beneficent one, to remove the causes which, if unremoved, might lead to a resort to arms. The safest and surest means to prevent war is to minimize the causes of war and to remove, as far as possible, its pretexts. Justice, as administered in municipal courts, has done away with the principle of self-help and the use of force as a means of redress. An international court where justice is administered equally and impartially to the small as well as to the great will go far to substitute the rule of law for the rule of man, order for disorder, equilibrium for instability, peace and content for disorder and apprehension of the future. To employ the language of a distinguished colleague, M. de Martens, the line of progress is *par la justice vers la paix*.

(3) MR. LÉON BOURGEOIS' REMARKS AT THE SESSION OF AUGUST 3, 1907, OF THE FIRST SUBCOMMISSION OF THE FIRST COMMISSION [1]

I have listened to the objections which have been so eloquently and forcibly urged by a number of our colleagues against the projects for the establishment of a Permanent Court of Arbitration, presented by the delegations of the United States and of Russia, and I have noted their misgivings, which must be given most careful consideration. It seems to me, however, that we can reassure them.

I share the views of Sir Edward Fry and the Marquis of Soveral, and I would state that, if the propositions which we are examining were likely to result in the abolition of the Court of Arbitration, as established at The Hague in 1899, these propositions would have no more determined opponent than I myself. Mr. Beernaert has done me the great honor to quote the words that I have repeatedly used to express my devotion to the principles of the First Conference and to defend the system of 1899 and the appointment of arbitrators by the parties. I find nothing to retract in what I have said. I still think what I thought at the time of the general organization of a universal court of arbitration, when its jurisdiction is considered as a whole and when it is a question of throwing it open to all international disputes, even the gravest. But the question today is entirely different; the question is whether, in certain restricted cases, under special conditions, it is not possible to make arbitration a more rapid and easier process, under a new form, but one that is in no way incompatible with its first form.

It was in this spirit that the French delegation, which has already submitted two propositions aiming to facilitate access to and simplify the procedure of the international courts of The Hague, examined with open mind the propositions of the United States and of Russia, and in this spirit it now gives its cordial support to the ideas which inspired them. We are all animated by a desire to further the cause of arbitration; but we appear to be divided into two groups when we try to find the method that will best increase its application. Two systems are face to face: The first consists in proclaiming arbitration compulsory in certain cases; the second is based upon the *permanence* of a strongly constituted tribunal. For our part, we believe that these two methods should not be separated.

We admit the force of certain criticisms directed by Mr. Asser and Mr. Choate against the institution of 1899. As Mr. Asser said, "There must be judges at The Hague." If there are none here now, it is because the Conference of 1899, surveying the whole field open to arbitrations, meant to leave it to the parties to choose their judges, a choice that is essential in all cases of a certain serious nature. We would not like to see the truly arbitral character of the Court of 1899 disappear, and we mean to maintain the free choice of judges as the higher and common rule in all cases for which no other rule has been stipulated. In disputes of a political nature especially we believe that this rule shall always be the real rule of arbitration, and that no state, small or great, will consent to go before an arbitral tribunal unless it has taken an active part in the appointment of the members composing this tribunal.

[1] Deuxième Conférence de la Paix, Actes et Documents, Vol. II, pp. 347-349.

But does the same thing hold with respect to questions of a purely legal nature? Can there be the same misgivings, the same distrust? And does not everyone perceive that a real court composed of real jurists may be the most competent agency to decide disputes of this kind and to render decisions upon questions which are purely questions of law? It is our opinion, therefore, that the older system of 1899 or the newer system of a truly permanent court may be preferred according to the nature of the cases. At any rate, there is no question of making the new system compulsory; no one will be forced to utilize the one rather than the other. The choice between the Court of 1899 and the Tribunal of 1907 will be optional. As Sir Edward Fry has well said: "Experience will bring out the advantages or the drawbacks of the two systems. Usage will best sanction the jurisdiction of each."

If we have admitted, gentlemen, that it is impossible to extend the jurisdiction of a permanent court to all cases of arbitration, we shall likewise be compelled to admit that it is impossible to subject all these cases to arbitration, whatever form this jurisdiction may be given. Some states, indeed—Italy and Denmark, for example—have found it possible to make general treaties of compulsory arbitration with each other, including, without any reservation, all cases, even political disputes. But who in the present state of the world can hope to see all the nations sign a universal convention, including political disputes?

Here again we are led to draw a distinction between political questions and legal questions, which a while ago enlightened and guided us. In the matter of political disputes it does not at this time appear to be possible to make arbitration compulsory by means of a universal treaty. On the other hand, however, is not the obligation to resort to arbitration in differences of a purely legal nature, for which no one of them would want to risk a bloody conflict, acceptable to all states? In this field we can hope to draw the bonds of arbitration around the nations; we can hope that they will consent to recognize the obligation. And when I say obligation, I mean a real obligation without reservations; because, in the matter of legal questions, I reject, as does Baron Marschall, the so-called clause of "honor and vital interests." All jurists will agree that these words introduce a "potestative condition" into conventions, whereby they lose the character of a legal necessity and the engagement is stripped of its force. Where the obligation is possible it must be made a reality.

Therefore, gentlemen, we see before us two distinct spheres—the sphere of permanence and the sphere of obligation. But in both spheres we reach the same conclusions. There is in the sphere of universal arbitration a zone of possible obligation and a zone of necessary option. There are a number of political questions which, in the present state of the world, cannot be subjected to universal, compulsory arbitration. Likewise in the sphere of permanence there are matters which by their very nature may be, perhaps ought to be, submitted to a permanent tribunal. That is to say, there are matters for which a permanent tribunal is possible; but there are other matters for which the system of 1899 continues to be necessary, for it alone can give the states the confidence and security without which they will not come before arbitrators.

Now, it is found that the cases which can be referred to the permanent tribunal are *the same* as those for which compulsory arbitration is acceptable. On the other hand, political matters, for which the states must continue to have the privilege of resorting to arbitration, are precisely those which require arbitrators rather than judges, arbitrators chosen with a free hand at the very time that the dispute arises. Do we not now perceive, by adequate analysis, the exact status of the problem? And is it not the very nature of the things themselves that furnishes us with the solution?

Is it possible, gentlemen, to reach an agreement whereby this problem may be given life? Still keeping intact this great Court of 1899, whose services are already recorded in history, can we establish alongside of it—perhaps within it—a more limited tribunal, truly permanent and truly legal in character, for purely legal cases? Is it possible to reach an agreement wherein we shall declare that purely legal cases are subject to compulsory arbitration? May we thus strengthen and fix in part, as it were, the international institution of arbitration, both with respect to its judges and with respect to the questions over which it has jurisdiction? We hope so, and we shall hail with joy the day when, alongside of the Court of 1899, or better, at its very hearth, and perhaps by it, a permanent court may be constituted for matters of a purely legal nature, under such conditions that the smallest as well as the greatest states may find in it equal guarantees for the defining and security of their rights.

It has been justly said that in the other commissions of the Conference questions pertaining to the regulation of war have been considered especially. Even in our First Commission, the subcommission in which, on the initiative of our colleagues of Germany and England, the very interesting project of a Prize Court is being elaborated, is in reality engaged upon a court for times of war. Here alone in our subcommission we can endeavor to diminish the danger of war, to strengthen peace. We have seen that there are at present two practical methods of accomplishing this, and we have said that in our opinion these two methods are inseparable—on the one hand the defining of a certain number of cases, where there is a real obligation to submit them to arbitration, and on the other hand the establishment of a truly permanent court. We shall labor with all our might to bring about this two-fold result.

The world wants peace. For centuries only one formula has been believed in, " Si vis pacem, para bellum"; that is to say, we have confined ourselves to the military organization of peace. We are no longer there, but we should not consider it sufficient to bring about the more human organization—I was about to say the pacific organization—of war.

The debates which have taken place here have shown us the progress of education in this matter, the new and ever-growing sentiment of the solidarity of nations and of men in the struggle against natural fatalities. We have confidence in the increasing activity of these great moral forces, and we hope that the Conference of 1907 will cause the work undertaken in 1899 to take a decisive step forward by insuring, in a practical and real manner, the legal organization of peace. [Repeated applause.]

(4) MR. CHOATE'S ADDRESS ON THE COMPOSITION OF THE PROPOSED COURT OF ARBITRAL JUSTICE, SEPTEMBER 5, 1907.[1]

The committee has now reached a stage in its deliberations which marks a most important advance towards the creation of a permanent court of arbitration which shall satisfy the universal demand that presses upon us. We have decided with practical unanimity that there shall be such a court, and have adopted a constitution for its organization and powers with equal unanimity. It is true that the representatives of several powers have declined to take part in the discussions involved in the second reading of the *projet* until they should know what plan would be adopted for determining the number of the judges of the court and the mode of their partition among the nations. But I do not understand that even those nations find any objection to any feature of the *projet*, and, in fact, the observations which fell from them, and their acquiescence in the action of the committee on the first reading of the *projet*, manifested an entire approval of it.

If the conference could do no more than this, it would have made very marked progress in the work, for in the First Conference the very idea of the creation of such a court was promptly laid aside as impracticable, if not impossible. But we owe it to ourselves, and to the nations that we represent, not to let the work stop here, but, by a supreme effort for conciliation, to agree upon the important and vital subject of determining the number of judges and the mode of their distribution and the measure of their action. Whether we do this permanently or provisionally is not of very great consequence. To accomplish it in either way will make the conference a great success. If we fail to bring it about in one way or the other, the conference itself will be to that extent a failure. And having come to The Hague accredited by the nations that sent us, we shall return to them seriously discredited.

It may, therefore, not be out of place for me, who originally introduced the proposition for the court—which up to this point has been sustained with such general favor—to review very briefly the various suggestions that have been made on this important subject.

When the subcommittee that had in charge the preparation of the *projet*, consisting of one from each of the delegations—British, German, and American— had completed it, they attempted to devise a scheme, a possible scheme, which should serve as a basis of discussion and challenge the presentation of any and every other scheme that any member of the committee might regard as possible. It was not even recommended by them for adoption, nor was it in any sense a joint scheme of the three powers or a separate scheme of either—American, British, or German. It recognized and was based upon the equal sovereignty of the nations, and took account at the same time of the differences that existed between them in population, in territory, in commerce, in language, in systems of

[1] La Deuxième Conférence Internationale de la Paix, Actes et Documents (1st Commission, Committee of Examination B, September 5, 1907), Vol. II, pp. 683-687 (689-693).

law, and in other respects, and especially the difference in the interests which the several nations would normally and naturally have at stake in the proceedings before the court and in the exercise of its jurisdiction. It provided for a court of seventeen judges, to be organized for a period of twelve years, and that of the seventeen, eight nations, who will be generally recognized as having the greatest interests at stake in the exercise by the court of its powers, should each have a judge sitting during the whole period of the organization.

It provided also that each of the other powers should appoint, in the same way and at the same time, a judge for the same period, but who should be called to the exercise of judicial functions in the court for variously measured periods, according to their population, territorial extent, commerce, and probable interest at stake before the court, these measured periods ranging from ten years down to one.

By this method the absolute and equal sovereignty of each of the forty-five powers was duly respected and their differences in other respects not lost sight of.

The presentation and distribution of this scheme, as an anonymous one, has answered the purpose of inviting abundant criticism and the presentation of counter-schemes. The main objection to it, held by many of the nations to whom it assigned less than a full period for the exercise of judicial functions by their judges, has been that the failure to give to the judges appointed by each nation full power to sit all the time was in some way a derogation from the dignity and sovereignty of each of them, and that the same principle which recognized the equal sovereignty of each of the forty-five nations required a recognition of the claim that they were equal in all other respects. This claim, if insisted and acted upon, would of course render the establishment of an international court on any such basis of partition an absolute impossibility, and require a court of forty-five judges sitting all the time.

As was expected, a very interesting counter-scheme was proposed, based upon the alleged equality, not only in sovereignty but in all other respects, of all the states. It proposed to abolish the existing court, and for a new court to be constituted, consisting of forty-five judges, one to be appointed by each state, and these to be divided into groups in alphabetical order, of fifteen each, which were to sit for alternate periods of three years. This scheme was offered as an illustration of what was possible, based upon a recognition of the absolute equality of all states. Two objections to it were suggested: First, that an allotment of periods by alphabetical order was really the creation of a court by chance; and second, that it deprived each nation of any hand or voice in the court for six years out of the nine for which it proposed to establish it; whereas the first scheme had given every nation a seat in the court by a permanent judge for a fixed period, besides the right to have a judge of its own appointment upon the court whenever it had a case before it for decision.

Another proposal has been that seventeen nations, including the eight first mentioned and nine others which together should represent all parts of the world, all languages, systems of law, races, and human interests, should be selected by the conference, with a power to each to appoint a judge for the whole term of the court, thus recognizing the principle of equality of sovereignty to be exercised in the power of creating the court and selecting the judges.

Another proposal has been that four judges should be assigned to America, as a unit, trusting to that cordial and friendly relation which exists at the present time, and it is hoped will always exist, between the United States and all other nations of Central and South America, and which has been successfully fostered and maintained by several Pan-American conferences, to enable them to make a distribution among themselves of the four judges so assigned, in a manner that should be satisfactory to all.

This plan would have relieved the problem of all questions raised in regard to America, and would have left it for the other nations to make a similar distribution of the thirteen judges among themselves, which it was hoped might be done by means of the peaceful and friendly relations now existing between all the nations of both continents.

The practicability of this scheme, as of all the others, is still open for the consideration of the committee.

The suggestion has also been made that, for the purpose of the partition of the judges of the court, the nations should be classified upon the sole element of comparative population; but it has been found, upon examination, that there were so many other essential factors that ought, upon every principle of justice and common sense, to enter into the distribution of judges that no definite project for such a distribution has been proposed.

The statements already made demonstrate the extreme delicacy and difficulty of the problem presented to the conference in the formation of the Permanent Court, but I confidently believe that it is entirely within the power of the committee, on a frank and candid exchange of views, and with the disposition that possesses it, to make such mutual concessions as may be necessary to solve the problem.

It has been suggested that it would be better to put the several plans proposed to the vote, so as to draw the line of distinction clearly between its advocates and its opponents; but, as all are believed to be in favor of the Permanent Court, the expediency of such a proposition is doubtful, for such a vote would not in any way indicate what nations were in favor of a permanent court and which of them were opposed. And to have the project of a court voted down because linked with a scheme for the distribution of judges that was unacceptable to a majority would convey to the world a wrong impression—that the conference was not in favor of the creation of such a court.

It has also been suggested that the difficulty should be regarded as insuperable in the present conference, and avoided, or rather evaded, by securing a unanimous vote for the establishment of the court upon the constitution now under consideration, and leaving it to the powers or to the next conference to establish, if possible, a mode of selecting the judges that should be satisfactory to all the powers.

As I have already said, the adoption of this plan would be perhaps an advance upon anything that has heretofore been accomplished. But it would be surely a serious failure, and should not be resorted to with any false illusions, as it might practically result in the burial of the project for a permanent court altogether.

We must solve the problem—either permanently or provisionally. This is a solemn duty that rests upon us, and it would be ignominious in the last degree for us to confess our inability to discharge it; and we therefore have to consider a wholly different method from any of those heretofore suggested, namely, a free election by the whole conference, voting by states, each exercising sovereign power on an absolute equality, and accepting the result of such an election, as electors or elected, as such an exercise of the elective power might produce.

There is nothing to prevent the conference voting freely and without any restraint whatever for a definite number of nations—seven or nine or eleven, thirteen or seventeen—who should each be authorized to appoint a judge for the full term of the court. This would concede all that is claimed in the way not only of equal sovereignty but of equality in all other respects, and each nation would take its chance of a successful canvass, and I have no doubt it would result in the successful establishment of an excellent court to which all nations could resort or refrain from resorting in each case that should arise, as they should see fit.

Another plan worthy of consideration, and which, I think, might successfully solve the problem, is to resort to an election—in which all the states should have an equal voice—of individuals, jurists, or statesmen of distinction, to constitute the court. If this method is resorted to, it might be in connection with the plan for establishing the court and its constitution, and leaving the method of final and permanent selection of judges to the nations or to the next conference. For it might and perhaps ought to be resorted to as a temporary and provisional plan to secure the organization of the court as soon as it should be ratified by a sufficient number of powers constituting a majority.

The plan would be for an election, each state casting one vote, of a prescribed number of judges, which should be deemed suitable for the temporary and provisional organization of the court, to hold office either until the next conference or for a specified number of years, or until the powers, by a diplomatic interchange of views, should adopt some different method as a permanency.

There is ample material within the conference itself and within the existing court, in the constitution of which all the powers have had an equal hand, for the creation and installation of such a tribunal provisionally. The selection might be limited to the members of the existing court, or extended to other jurists whose names are familiar to all, every one of them of the highest character and of world-wide reputation, and any quorum of whom, sitting as a court, would command the confidence and admiration of the entire world, and be relied upon to do justice in any case that might arise. For one, speaking for the United States of America, I should be perfectly willing to intrust the fortunes of the court, and the success of this conference in creating it, to the result of any election that might be made as suggested, and I hope that it will be taken into serious consideration and recommended for action by the committee, in the event of no plan being proposed that can command more general approval.

A further method of election, under further limitations, has been proposed and is also worthy of consideration, and that is that the nations should nominate each a number of jurists, selected from the old court or at large, to constitute the new court, whether provisionally or permanently; that these nominations should be received by an executive committee of three, to be appointed by the president of the conference; and that the names of all candidates nominated by five or more powers should be placed upon a ballot and offered for the final choice of the conference, voting by states; and that those receiving the largest number of votes on such final ballot, to the requisite number prescribed for the court, should be declared the elected judges.

I am not without hope that still other plans will be evolved from the discussion of this intricate and important matter which is now to take place that may command the approval of the committee and secure the establishment of the court.

So sure am I that the establishment and organization of the court will be a great triumph of civilization and justice, and an effectual guarantee of the peace of the world, that I would urge, with all the earnestness of which I am capable, the adoption even of one of the provisional schemes referred to, if no permanent method for the choice of judges can be now agreed upon. And I trust that, laying aside all prejudices and national differences, all pride of opinion and all desire to secure special advantages for our respective nations, we shall devote ourselves, with one mind and one heart, to the solution of the problem that is now before us.

(5) MR. CHOATE'S REMARKS ON THE SELECTION OF THE JUDGES
OF THE COURT OF ARBITRAL JUSTICE BY THE PRINCIPLE
OF ELECTION, SEPTEMBER 18, 1907 [1]

I do not think that the time has come to give ourselves up to despair. We must do something to realize the hopes of the civilized world.

It follows from the speech of M. Barbosa that he objects to accepting any other plan than his own. That is another form of despair. But in any case, as the president has very clearly shown, the investigating committee has not yet decided the question.

Many plans have been presented to this committee, but they have not been sufficiently studied and discussed.

I persist in thinking that the *plan of rotation* would be the cleverest and the most just. However, in face of the opposition of certain powers, we have given it up.

The only method which, under the present conditions, offers any chance of success is therefore that of the *election* of a court, whether it be a permanent or a provisional one.

The objections made to this method of composition of the court are purely imaginary. It is the laying down of distrust as a principle—the distrust of the wisdom and of the loyalty of the electors.

One fears the coalitions of small powers against the great. I declare that I do not share these apprehensions.

The representatives of the small nations are as qualified to be electors as the others, and they will agree to choose the best judges, independently of nationality. And assuredly, worthy judges can be found among the subjects of these small nations. If we have not confidence in each other, why do we strive, then, to conclude a convention? Why do we not adopt a method which admits the principle of the equality of nations?

For myself, personally, I would run the risk of an election, whether it be made by the governments, or by the Permanent Court, or by this same conference, provided that all nationalities, all languages, and all systems of law be represented. It matters little to me whether my nation may have a judge or not. We are not here for the sole advantage of our own country, but for the benefit of the community of nations.

The plan of M. de Martens, which has been submitted to us, is excellent as a whole. He proposes that each country designate an elector, taken from the list of the members of the Permanent Court, and that these forty-five electors should, in their turn, choose fifteen judges, who should form the court.

Nevertheless, in this plan a certain number of judges is ascribed to Europe, to America, and to Asia, and that is its vulnerable point, for that recalls to mind the old plan of rotation. On the other hand, it does not appear indispensable to assemble again all the electors at The Hague, for practically the vote would

[1] La Deuxième Conférence Internationale de la Paix, Actes et Documents (1st Commission, Committee of Examination B, September 18, 1907), Vol. II, pp. 697-699.

be issued by the governments. One could therefore dispense with the formality of the reunion and have the electors vote through the medium of the bureau.[1]

I take the liberty in this class of ideas to make a proposition to the committee which seems to me to answer all of the objections.

PROPOSITION WITH REGARD TO THE COMPOSITION OF THE COURT OF ARBITRAL JUSTICE

ARTICLE 1. Every signatory power shall have the privilege of appointing a judge and an assistant qualified for and disposed to accept such positions and to transmit the names to the international bureau.

ARTICLE 2. The bureau, that being the case, shall make a list of all the proposed judges and assistants, with indication of the nations proposing them, and shall transmit it to all the signatory powers.

ARTICLE 3. Each signatory power shall signify to the bureau which one of the judges and assistants thus named it chooses, each nation voting for fifteen judges and fifteen assistants at the same time.

ARTICLE 4. The bureau, on receiving the list thus voted for, shall make out a list of the names of the fifteen judges and of the fifteen assistants having received the greatest number of votes.

ARTICLE 5. In the case of an equality of votes affecting the selection of the fifteen judges and the fifteen assistants, the choice between them shall be by a drawing by lot made by the bureau.

ARTICLE 6. In case of vacancy arising in a position of judge or of assistant, the vacancy shall be filled by the nation to which the judge or assistant belonged.

This plan is so simple that there is no need of long discussion. If fifteen nations only accept it, it could become the point of departure of a general agreement. The example of 1899 is there to prove that the adhesions could come afterwards.

The immediate adhesion of any particular nation, great or small, would not be indispensable. This would be an experiment, and the nations who would not accept it to-day would be able to come to a decision later on.

I think that my proposition, if it is adopted, will give us good judges and will satisfy all the world.

It is a matter of indifference to me whether the election takes place here or elsewhere, whether the court be permanent or provisional, constituted for five, for three, for two years, provided that we may not return to our countries with empty hands. It is better to do something than to do nothing. I do not yet share the despair which some of the delegates who support our plan have expressed. As long as the conference lives there is cause for hope.

---

[1] The institution referred to is the international bureau, which is the record office of the so-called Permanent Court and "the channel for communications relative to the meetings of the court"—(Convention of 1899, for the Pacific Settlement of International Disputes, Art. 23; Revision of 1907, Art. 44).

APPENDIX B

(1) THE AMERICAN PROJECT FOR A PERMANENT COURT OF ARBITRATION.[1]

I. A Permanent Court of Arbitration shall be organized, to consist of fifteen judges of the highest moral standing and of recognized competency in questions of international law. They and their successors shall be appointed in the manner to be determined by this Conference, but they shall be so chosen from the different countries that the various systems of law and procedure and the principal languages shall be suitably represented in the personnel of the court. They shall be appointed for ——— years, or until their successors have been appointed and have accepted.

II. The Permanent Court shall convene annually at The Hague on a specified date and shall remain in session as long as necessary. It shall elect its own officers and, saving the stipulations of the convention, it shall draw up its own regulations. Every decision shall be reached by a majority, and nine members shall constitute a quorum. The judges shall be equal in rank, shall enjoy diplomatic immunity, and shall receive a salary sufficient to enable them to devote their time to the consideration of the matters brought before them.

III. In no case (unless the parties expressly consent thereto) shall a judge take part in the consideration or decision of any case before the court when his nation is a party therein.

IV. The Permanent Court shall be competent to take cognizance and determine all cases involving differences of an international character between sovereign nations, which it has been impossible to settle through diplomatic channels and which have been submitted to it by agreement between the parties, either originally or for review or revision, or in order to determine the relative rights, duties or obligations in accordance with the finding, decisions, or awards of commissions of inquiry and specifically constituted tribunals of arbitration.

V. The judges of the Permanent Court shall be competent to act as judges in any Commission of Inquiry or Special Tribunal of Arbitration which may be constituted by any power for the consideration of any matter which may be specially referred to it and which must be determined by it.

VI. The present Permanent Court of Arbitration might, as far as possible, constitute the basis of the court, care being taken that the powers which recently signed the Convention of 1899 are represented in it.

[1] La Deuxième Conférence Internationale de la Paix, Actes et Documents, Vol. II, pp. 1031-1032; Scott's Hague Peace Conferences of 1899 and 1907, pp. 821-822.

(2) THE PROJECT FOR A PERMANENT COURT OF ARBITRATION DRAFTED BY THE AMERICAN DELEGATION UPON WHICH THE JOINT PROJECT OF GERMANY, GREAT BRITAIN AND THE UNITED STATES WAS BASED.[1]

ARTICLE 1. With the object of facilitating an immediate recourse to arbitration for international differences which could not be settled by diplomatic methods, the signatory powers undertake to organize a Permanent Court of Arbitration accessible at all times, and acting, unless otherwise stipulated by the parties, in accordance with the rules of procedure included in the present convention.

ARTICLE 2. The Permanent Court of Arbitration shall be composed of fifteen (sixteen) persons possessing the qualifications required for judges in their respective countries, and who shall be of known competency in questions of international law.

The judges of the Permanent Court of Arbitration shall hold office for the period of . . . . (six) years, or until their successors are appointed and qualify.

The judges of the Permanent Court of Arbitration herein provided for shall be chosen as far as practicable from the list of members comprising the existing court.

ARTICLE 3. In case of the expiration of the term of office, death, resignation, inability to act, or failure to qualify, of any judge, the vacancy shall be filled by the state or group of states having the right to appoint the said judge and in accordance with the provisions of the article governing appointments. The successor so appointed shall be, if practicable, selected from the list of members of the existing Court of Arbitration.

ARTICLE 4. The judges of the Permanent Court of Arbitration shall be appointed and sworn, or shall otherwise qualify, according to the law of their respective states regulating the duties and obligations of judicial officers. The appointment, acceptance and oath of office taken by the judge shall be certified to the Administrative Council by the appointing state. The commissions of the judges of the Permanent Court of Arbitration shall be in the form prescribed by the Administrative Council and the judges so commissioned shall be accredited to the said council.

ARTICLE 5. In no case (unless the party in controversy shall expressly consent thereto) shall a judge participate in the consideration or discussion of any matter before the Permanent Court of Arbitration in which his state is a party.

ARTICLE 6. Each judge of the Permanent Court of Arbitration shall, during his term of office, receive an annual compensation of . . . to be borne by the signatory powers in the proportion established for the International Bureau of the Universal Postal Union.

The salary herein specified shall be paid by the International Bureau at the expiration of each six months from the date of the opening of the Permanent Court of Arbitration at The Hague.

The judges of the Permanent Court of Arbitration shall be reimbursed by the International Bureau for the necessary traveling expenses upon the approval of the Administrative Council.

No judge or officer of the Permanent Court of Arbitration shall receive from his own or any other state any compensation or allowance for his services on the Permanent Court or Special Arbitration, Commission of Inquiry, or any matter whatever connected with the exercise of his duties as judge of the Permanent Court of Arbitration.

ARTICLE 7. The court shall meet annually at The Hague (on the third Wednesday in June) and shall remain in session for a period of sixty days and such longer time as shall be necessary for the disposal of business before it.

[1] Reprinted from Scott's " American Addresses " at the Second Hague Peace Conference, p. 206.

Nine judges of the Permanent Court of Arbitration shall constitute a quorum for the transaction of business, and all decisions shall be by a majority vote of those present and participating.

The Permanent Court of Arbitration may adjourn to a fixed date, or it may adjourn to reassemble upon the call of the president in order to consider or receive matters which may be presented for its consideration.

ARTICLE 8. The judges of the Permanent Court of Arbitration shall be of equal rank, and be entitled to diplomatic immunity. They shall choose a presiding judge from among their number and they shall be seated according to the date of their respective commissions.

The presiding judge shall be the president of the Permanent Court of Arbitration, and in the performance of his duties shall exercise no greater authority and prerogatives than the judges of the Permanent Court, unless such have been specially conferred upon him by the judges of said court.

ARTICLE 9. The International Bureau of the Court of Arbitration of The Hague shall serve as the Secretariat of the Permanent Court of Arbitration. It shall have custody of the archives and of the proceedings of the Permanent Court of Arbitration.

All communications between the Permanent Court of Arbitration and the powers, except those made in open court, shall be through the International Bureau.

ARTICLE 10. The Permanent Court of Arbitration shall make rules of procedure not inconsistent with nor prescribed by the Convention for the Peaceful Settlement of International Differences.

ARTICLE 11. The Permanent Court of Arbitration shall be competent to receive, consider and determine any claim or petition from a sovereign state touching any difference of an international character with another sovereign state which diplomacy has failed to settle; provided, however, that such difference is not political in character and does not involve the honor, independence or vital interests of any state.

It shall also be competent to receive and consider any application from a sovereign state to review and revise or determine the relative rights, duties and liabilities under the findings rendered within one year by any Commission of Inquiry or Special Arbitration between sovereign states to which the petitioning state was a party.

ARTICLE 12. The Permanent Court of Arbitration shall not be competent to receive or consider any petition, application or communication whatever from any person natural or artificial except a sovereign state, nor shall it be competent to receive any application or petition from any sovereign state unless it relates exclusively to a difference of an international character with another state which diplomacy has failed to settle and which is not political in character and does not affect the honor, independence or vital interests of any state.

ARTICLE 13. The Permanent Court of Arbitration shall not take any action on any petition or application which it is competent to receive unless it shall be of the opinion that a justiciable case, and one which it is competent to entertain and decide and worthy of its consideration, has been brought before it, in which case it may in not less than thirty or more than ninety days after presentation of the petition invite the other sovereign state to appear and submit the matter to judicial determination by the court.

In the latter event the state so invited may (a) refuse to submit the matter, (b) refrain from submitting the matter by failing for . . . days to make any response to the invitation, in which event it shall be deemed to have refused to submit the matter; (c) submit the matter in whole, or (d) offer to submit the matter in part or in different form from that stated in the petition, in which event the petitioning state shall be free either to accept the qualified submission or to withdraw its petition or application, and shall signify its election within a time to be determined by the court; (e) appear for the sole purpose of denying the right of the petitioning state to any redress or relief on the petition or application presented—that is to say, it may except or demur; in case the court does not sustain this, it shall renew the invitation to appear and submit the matter.

ARTICLE 14. In case, however, the states in controversy cannot agree upon the form and scope of the submission of the difference referred to in the petition, the Court of Arbitration may appoint, upon the request by either party, a committee of three from the members of the Administrative Council, none of whom shall represent the states involved, without suggestion from either party, and the committee thus constituted shall frame the questions to be submitted and the scope of the inquiry, and thereafter if either party shall withdraw it shall be deemed to have refused to submit the matter involved to judicial or arbitral determination.

ARTICLE 15. The Administrative Council shall transmit to every signatory power a copy of every petition which may be submitted to the Permanent Court of Arbitration, and any power affected thereby shall have the right to present through the Administrative Council any matter bearing on the question involved which it sees fit to do, and any matter so presented shall be transmitted by the Administrative Council to every signatory power.

ARTICLE 16. An agreement to submit a controversy to or appearance and submission of the case in the Permanent Court of Arbitration implies an obligation to submit in good faith to the decision of the court on the question submitted.

ARTICLE 17. After a controversy has been submitted, the court may determine whether the testimony shall be taken by the court or by a commission, and in the latter case the court may delegate one or more of its judges or appoint commissioners to take the testimony; and, on consent of the parties, the court may direct where, when and how the testimony shall be taken and in what proportion the expense shall be borne, disbursed and apportioned; but except as otherwise stipulated, or in case the parties cannot agree, the procedure in taking testimony shall be the same as provided in Chapter . . . of the Convention for the Pacific Settlement of International Disputes, relating to commissions of inquiry, except that the testimony shall be transmitted to the court without expressions of opinion.

ARTICLE 18. If two powers agree to submit a difference to the Permanent Court of Arbitration and desire a summary hearing and determination, they may request a special detail either of three or of five judges, and may select the judges to compose the detail by striking alternately from the list of judges an equal number until the desired number shall remain.

Powers desiring to form a Commission of Inquiry for a particular purpose may resort to the Permanent Court of Arbitration and constitute the commission in the above described manner, and add thereto an equal number of nationals from each of the parties.

ARTICLE 19. The judges of the Permanent Court of Arbitration may constitute the division of the High Court of Prize established by Chapter . . . of this convention.

The personnel of the division of the High Court may be modified to meet the regulations and requirements of the convention creating the Court of Prize.

(3) DRAFT CONVENTION FOR THE ESTABLISHMENT OF THE COURT OF ARBITRAL JUSTICE [1]

Part I. Constitution of the Judicial Arbitration Court.

Article 1. With a view to promoting the cause of arbitration, the contracting powers agree to constitute, without altering the status of the Permanent Court of Arbitration, a Judicial Arbitration Court, of free and easy access, composed of judges representing the various juridical systems of the world, and capable of insuring continuity in jurisprudence of arbitration.

Article 2. The Judicial Arbitration Court is composed of judges and deputy judges chosen from persons of the highest moral reputation, and all fulfilling conditions qualifying them, in their respective countries, to occupy high legal posts, or be jurists of recognized competence in matters of international law.

The judges and deputy judges of the court are appointed, as far as possible, from the members of the Permanent Court of Arbitration. The appointment shall be made within the six months following the ratification of the present convention.

Article 3. The judges and deputy judges are appointed for a period of twelve years, counting from the date on which the appointment is notified to the Administrative Council created by the convention for the pacific settlement of international disputes. Their appointments can be renewed.

Should a judge or deputy judge die or retire, the vacancy is filled in the manner in which his appointment was made. In this case, the appointment is made for a fresh period of twelve years.

Article 4. The judges of the Judicial Arbitration Court are equal and rank according to the date on which their appointment was notified. The judge who is senior in point of age takes precedence when the date of notification is the same.

The deputy judges are assimilated, in the exercise of their functions, with the judges. They rank, however, below the latter.

Article 5. The judges enjoy diplomatic privileges and immunities in the exercise of their functions, outside their own country.

Before taking their seats, the judges and deputy judges must

---

[1] La Deuxième Conférence Internationale de la Paix, Actes et Documents, Vol. 1, pp. 702-707; Scott's Texts of the Peace Conferences at The Hague of 1899 and 1907, pp. 141-154.

swear, before the Administrative Council, or make a solemn affirmation to exercise their functions impartially and conscientiously.

Article 6. The court annually nominates three judges to form a special delegation and three more to replace them should the necessity arise. They may be re-elected. They are balloted for. The persons who secure the largest number of votes are considered elected. The delegation itself elects its president, who, in default of a majority, is appointed by lot.

A member of the delegation cannot exercise his duties when the power which appointed him, or of which he is a national, is one of the parties.

The members of the delegation are to conclude all matters submitted to them, even if the period for which they have been appointed judges has expired.

Article 7. A judge may not exercise his judicial functions in any case in which he has, in any way whatever, taken part in the decision of a national tribunal, of a tribunal of arbitration, or of a commission of inquiry, or has figured in the suit as counsel or advocate for one of the parties.

A judge cannot act as agent or advocate before the Judicial Arbitration Court or the Permanent Court of Arbitration, before a special tribunal of arbitration or a commission of inquiry, nor act for one of the parties in any capacity whatsoever as long as his appointment lasts.

Article 8. The court elects its president and vice-president by an absolute majority of the votes cast. After two ballots, the election is made by a bare majority and, in case the votes are even, by lot.

Article 9. The judges of the Judicial Arbitration Court receive an annual salary of 6,000 Netherland florins. This salary is paid at the end of each half year, reckoned from the date on which the court meets for the first time.

In the exercise of their duties during the sessions or in the special cases covered by the present convention, they receive the sum of 100 florins *per diem*. They are further entitled to receive a traveling allowance fixed in accordance with regulations existing in their own country. The provisions of the present paragraph are applicable also to a deputy judge when acting for a judge.

These emoluments are included in the general expenses of the court dealt with in Article 31, and are paid through the International Bureau created by the convention for the pacific settlement of international disputes.

Article 10. The judges may not accept from their own government or from that of any other power any remuneration for services connected with their duties in their capacity of members of the court.

Article 11. The seat of the Judicial Court of Arbitration is at The Hague, and cannot be transferred, unless absolutely obliged by circumstances, elsewhere.

The delegation may choose, with the assent of the parties concerned, another site for its meetings, if special circumstances render such a step necessary.

Article 12. The Administrative Council fulfills with regard to the Judicial Court of Arbitration the same functions as to the Permanent Court of Arbitration.

Article 13. The International Bureau acts as registry to the Judicial Court of Arbitration, and must place its offices and staff at the disposal of the court. It has charge of the archives and carries out the administrative work.

The Secretary-General of the Bureau discharges the functions of registrar.

The necessary secretaries to assist the registrar, translators and short-hand writers are appointed and sworn in by the court.

Article 14. The court meets in session once a year. The session opens the third Wednesday in June and lasts until all the business on the agenda has been transacted.

The court does not meet in session if the delegation considers that such meeting is unnecessary. However, when a power is party in a case actually pending before the court, the pleadings in which are closed, or about to be closed, it may insist that the session should be held.

When necessary, the delegation may summon the court in extraordinary session.

Article 15. A report of the doings of the court shall be drawn up every year by the delegation. This report shall be forwarded to the contracting powers through the International Bureau. It shall also be communicated to the judges and deputy judges of the court.

Article 16. The judges and deputy judges, members of the Judicial Arbitration Court, can also exercise the functions of judge and deputy judge in the International Prize Court.

Part II.   Competency and Procedure.

Article 17.   The Judicial Court of Arbitration is competent to deal with all cases submitted to it, in virtue either of a general undertaking to have recourse to arbitration or of a special agreement.

Article 18.   The delegation is competent:

1.   To decide the arbitration referred to in the preceding article, if the parties concerned are agreed that the summary procedure, laid down in Part IV, Chapter IV, of the convention for the pacific settlement of international disputes is to be applied;

2.   To hold an inquiry under and in accordance with Part III of the said convention, in so far as the delegation is intrusted with such inquiry by the parties acting in common agreement.   With the assent of the parties concerned, and as an exception to Article 7, paragraph 1, the members of the delegation who have taken part in the inquiry may sit as judges, if the case in dispute is submitted to the arbitration of the court or of the delegation itself.

Article 19.   The delegation is also competent to settle the *compromis* referred to in Article 52 of the convention for the pacific settlement of international disputes if the parties are agreed to leave it to the court.

It is equally competent to do so, even when the request is only made by one of the parties concerned, if all attempts have failed to reach an understanding through the diplomatic channel, in the case of—

1.   A dispute covered by a general treaty of arbitration concluded or renewed after the present convention has come into force providing for a *compromis* in all disputes, and not either explicitly or implicitly excluding the settlement of the *compromis* from the competence of the delegation.   Recourse cannot, however, be had to the court if the other party declares that in its opinion the dispute does not belong to the category of questions to be submitted to compulsory arbitration, unless the treaty of arbitration confers upon the Arbitration Tribunal the power of deciding this preliminary question.

2.   A dispute arising from contract debts claimed from one power by another power as due to its nationals, and for the settlement of which the offer of arbitration has been accepted.   This arrangement is not applicable if acceptance is subject to the condition that the *compromis* should be settled in some other way.

Article 20. Each of the parties concerned may nominate a judge of the court to take part, with power to vote, in the examination of the case submitted to the delegation.

If the delegation acts as a commission of inquiry, this task may be intrusted to persons other than the judges of the court. The traveling expenses and remuneration to be given to the said persons are fixed and borne by the powers appointing them.

Article 21. The contracting powers only may have access to the Judicial Arbitration Court set up by the present convention.

Article 22. The Judicial Court of Arbitration follows the rules of procedure laid down in the convention for the pacific settlement of international disputes, except in so far as the procedure is laid down in the present convention.

Article 23. The court determines what language it will itself use and what languages may be used before it.

Article 24. The International Bureau serves as channel for all communications to be made to the judges during the interchange of pleadings provided for in Article 63, paragraph 2, of the convention for the pacific settlement of international disputes.

Article 25. For all notices to be served, in particular on the parties, witnesses or experts, the court may apply direct to the government of the state on whose territory the service is to be carried out. The same rule applies in the case of steps being taken to procure evidence.

The requests addressed for this purpose can only be rejected when the power applied to considers them likely to impair its sovereign rights or its safety. If the request is complied with, the fees charged must only comprise the expenses actually incurred.

The court is equally entitled to act through the power on whose territory it sits.

Notices to be given to parties in the place where the court sits may be served through the International Bureau.

Article 26. The discussions are under the control of the President or Vice-President, or, in case they are absent or cannot act, of the senior judge present.

The judge appointed by one of the parties cannot preside.

Article 27. The court considers its decisions in private, and the proceedings are secret.

All decisions are arrived at by a majority of the judges present. If the number of judges is even and equally divided, the vote of the junior judge, in the order of precedence laid down in Article 4, paragraph 1, is not counted.

Article 28. The judgment of the court must give the reasons on which it is based. It contains the names of the judges taking part in it; it is signed by the president and registrar.

Article 29. Each party pays its own costs and an equal share of the costs of the trial.

Article 30. The provisions of Articles 21 to 29 are applicable by analogy to the procedure before the delegation.

When the right of attaching a member to the delegation has been exercised by one of the parties only, the vote of the member attached is not recorded if the votes are evenly divided.

Article 31. The general expenses of the court are borne by the contracting powers.

The Administrative Council applies to the powers to obtain the funds requisite for the working of the court.

Article 32. The court itself draws up its own rules of procedure, which must be communicated to the contracting powers.

After the ratification of the present convention, the court shall meet as early as possible in order to elaborate these rules, elect the President and Vice-President and appoint the members of the delegation.

Article 33. The court may propose modifications in the provisions of the present convention concerning procedure. These proposals are communicated through the Netherland Government to the contracting powers, which will consider together as to the measures to be taken.

Part III. Final Provisions.

Article 34. The present convention shall be ratified as soon as possible.

The ratifications shall be deposited at The Hague.

A *proces-verbal* of the deposit of each ratification shall be drawn up, of which a duly certified copy shall be sent through the diplomatic channel to all the signatory powers.

Article 35. The convention shall come into force six months after its ratification.

It shall remain in force for twelve years, and shall be tacitly renewed for periods of twelve years, unless denounced.

The denunciation must be notified, at least two years before the expiration of each period, to the Netherland Government, which will inform the other powers.

The denunciation shall only have effect in regard to the notifying power. The convention shall continue in force as far as the other powers are concerned.

(4) *PROPOSAL FOR ESTABLISHMENT OF A COURT OF ARBITRAL JUSTICE BY AND FOR GERMANY, THE UNITED STATES, AUSTRIA-HUNGARY, FRANCE, GREAT BRITAIN, ITALY, JAPAN, THE NETHERLANDS, RUSSIA.*

His Majesty, the German Emperor, King of Prussia, etc.:

Considering that the Second Peace Conference, in the Final Act of October 18, 1907, recommended to the Signatory Powers the adoption of the draft, appended to said act, of a convention for the establishment of a Court of Arbitral Justice and the putting it into force as soon as an agreement should be reached on the choice of the judges and the organization of the court;

Being desirous of contributing toward the realization of the recommendation thus expressed;

Deeming that, if it is impossible as yet to reach a general agreement for putting into force the draft thus recommended, it is nevertheless useful to establish a Court of Arbitral Justice for such powers as may be willing to co-operate in its establishment and which may operate pending subsequent permanent rules;

Being persuaded that such a measure, essentially provisional, does not in any way prejudice any agreement which may be reached later for the permanent organization of the Court of Arbitral Justice, and that such an agreement is particularly likely to be reached at the Third Peace Conference;

Have decided to conclude a convention to insure the putting into force of the aforementioned draft, and have appointed as their plenipotentiaries, to wit:

Who, after depositing their full powers, found to be in due and proper form, have agreed upon the following provisions:

ARTICLE I

The contracting powers agree to put into force the draft, appended to the Final Act of the Second Peace Conference, of a convention relating to the establishment of a Court of Arbitral Justice, making thereto the necessary additions as stated below. The said draft, thereby made the standing rules binding the con-

tracting parties, is appended to the present convention and forms an integral part thereof.

ARTICLE 2.

The Court of Arbitral Justice shall be composed of nine judges, five constituting a quorum.

ARTICLE 3.

Each contracting power shall appoint a judge to serve during the life of the convention. The judges thus appointed take rank in accordance with the date of their assumption of office.

ARTICLE 4.

The Administrative Council referred to in Article 12 of the appended rules shall comprise the diplomatic representatives of the contracting powers accredited to The Hague and the Minister for Foreign Affairs of The Netherlands.

ARTICLE 5.

In derogation of Article 21 of the rules, action may be brought before the Court of Arbitral Justice and its delegation provided for in Article 6 of the rules, even by non-contracting powers.

If the controversy submitted to the Court of Arbitral Justice or its delegation be between a contracting and a non-contracting power, the latter shall have the right to appoint a judge to take part in the trial and determination of the case. If the powers in controversy be non-contracting powers, each one thereof shall have the right to appoint a judge to take part in the trial and determination of the case.

In such cases the remuneration of the judges appointed by the non-contracting power or powers shall be paid by the appointing power, and the expenses and fees caused by the trial and determination of the case submitted by a non-contracting power or powers shall be defrayed by the non-contracting power or powers to the extent determined by the court or its delegation, which shall take into account that one or both of the litigating parties is a non-contracting power, or that the court is convened especially for the case.

Article 6.

Notwithstanding the terms of Article 23 of the rules, the parties may, in every case, claim the right to use their own language.

Article 7.

The general expenses of the Court of Arbitral Justice shall be equally borne by the contracting powers.

The Administrative Council shall apply to the contracting powers in order to obtain the necessary funds for the operation of the court.

Article 8.

The present convention shall be ratified and the ratification deposited at The Hague as soon as seven powers shall be ready to ratify and can furnish to the court five judges.